THE BLIND GIANT IS DANCING

Stephen Sewell

Currency Press, Sydney

CURRENT THEATRE SERIES

First published in 1983
by Currency Press Pty Ltd,
PO Box 2287, Strawberry Hills, NSW, 2012, Australia
enquiries@currency.com.au
www.currency.com.au

This revised edition published in 2016 in association with Belvoir, Sydney.

Copyright: © Stephen Sewell, 1983, 1997, 2016.

COPYING FOR EDUCATIONAL PURPOSES

The Australian *Copyright Act 1968* (Act) allows a maximum of one chapter or 10% of this book, whichever is the greater, to be copied by any educational institution for its educational purposes provided that that educational institution (or the body that administers it) has given a remuneration notice to Copyright Agency Limited (CAL) under the Act.

For details of the CAL licence for educational institutions contact CAL, Level 15/233 Castlereagh Street, Sydney, NSW, 2000; tel: within Australia 1800 066 844 toll free; outside Australia 61 2 9394 7600; fax: 61 2 9394 7601; email: info@copyright.com.au

COPYING FOR OTHER PURPOSES

Except as permitted under the Act, for example a fair dealing for the purposes of study, research, criticism or review, no part of this book may be reproduced, stored in a retrieval system, or transmitted in any form or by any means without prior written permission. All enquiries should be made to the publisher at the address above.

Any performance or public reading of *The Blind Giant is Dancing* is forbidden unless a licence has been received from the author or the author's agent. The purchase of this book in no way gives the purchaser the right to perform the play in public, whether by means of a staged production or a reading. All applications for public performance should be addressed to The Yellow Agency, PO Box 736, Surry Hills NSW 2010, Australia; ph: 61 2 8090 4421; email: contact@theyellowagency.com

Cataloguing-in-publication data for this title is available from the National Library of Australia website: www.nla.gov.au

Typeset by Dean Nottle for Currency Press.
Cover design by Alphabet Studio.

Currency Press acknowledges the Traditional Owners of the Country on which we live and work. We pay our respects to all Aboriginal and Torres Strait Islander Elders, past and present.

Contents

THE BLIND GIANT IS DANCING

    Act One   1

    Act Two   32

    Act Three   68

Theatre Program at the end of the playtext

*To my friends
Anna Russell, Dan O'Neill and Marian Wilkinson*

*In memory of
Salvador Allende,
killed by fascist forces while defending the Moneda Palace
with his comrades, 11 September 1973*

'In these dark and bitter moments, where treachery claims to impose itself, you must know that sooner or later, and very soon, large avenues will again open for men worthy of building a new society.
Long live Chile!
Long live the People!
Long live the Workers!'

President Allende, 11 September 1973

The Blind Giant is Dancing was first produced by the State Theatre Company of South Australia, Adelaide, on 15 October 1983 with the following cast:

GRAHAM WHITE / BRUCE FITZGERALD	Russell Kiefel
MR CAREW / GREG	Robert Grubb
MICHAEL WELLS	Stuart McCreery
ALLEN FITZGERALD	Geoffrey Rush
LOUISE KRAUS	Jacqy Phillips
JANE	Robynne Bourne
ROSE DRAPER	Gillian Jones
JANICE LANG / ROBIN	Melita Jurisic
BOB LANG / SIR LESLIE HARRIS	John Wood
RAMON GRIS	Igor Sas
DOUG FITZGERALD	Peter Cummins
EILEEN FITZGERALD	Kerry Walker

Director, Neil Armfield
Designer, Stephen Curtis
Composer, Alan John
Lighting Designer, Nigel Levings

This revised version of the play was produced by Belvoir at the Belvoir St Theatre, Sydney, on 17 February 2016, with the following cast:

MR CAREW	Michael Denkha
RAMON GRIS	Ivan Donato
BRUCE FITZGERALD	Andrew Henry
JANICE / JANE / ROBIN	Emma Jackson
DOUG FITZGERALD / SIR LESLIE HARRIS	Russell Kiefel
EILEEN FITZGERALD	Genevieve Lemon
MICHAEL WELLS	Geoff Morrell
ROSE DRAPER	Zahra Newman
ALLEN FITZGERALD	Dan Spielman
LOUISE KRAUS	Yael Stone
BOB LANG	Ben Wood

Director, Eamon Flack
Set and Costume Designer, Dale Ferguson
Lighting Designer, Verity Hampson
Composer and Sound Designer, Steve Toulmin
Fight Choreographer, Scott Witt
Stage Manager, Melanie Stanton
Assistant Stage Manager, Grace Nye-Butler

CHARACTERS

GRAHAM WHITE, a criminal businessman
MICHAEL WELLS, a Social Democratic Party secretary and bureaucrat
MR CAREW, a Labour Hall functionary, American
ALLEN FITZGERALD, a social economist
LOUISE KRAUS, a feminist socialist, Allen's wife
JANE, a friend of Louise
ROSE DRAPER, a financial journalist
BOB LANG, a bourgeois economist and banker
JANICE LANG, wife of Bob
RAMON GRIS, a Chilean socialist exile
DOUG FITZGERALD, Allen's father, a steelworker
BRUCE FITZGERALD, Allen's brother, a steelworker
SIR LESLIE HARRIS, a capitalist
DIANNE, a secretary
GREG, a revolutionary
EILEEN FITZGERALD, Allen's mother
ROBIN, a worker at the women's refuge
PARTY GUESTS, THREE STEELWORKERS, FOUR THUGS

The characters and events in this drama are entirely fictitious. Any resemblance to any person alive or dead is coincidental.

This play went to press before the end of rehearsals and may differ from the play as performed.

ACT ONE

SCENE ONE

Blackout.

Fade up the sound of a glass wind bell. A slight pause: someone pushes their way through a bead curtain. Another pause: a moan in the darkness.

Fade up lights on a heavily-covered MAN—*unidentifiable. He appears to be looking through an expandable folder. A flopping sound, as of a man trying to rise. Fade up lights on a second man*—GRAHAM WHITE—*lying facedown on the floor. His head and shirt are covered with blood. He is moving.*

The unidentified MAN *moves to another folder.* WHITE *moans. There is a sudden tinkling of the wind bell as a gust moves it.*

WHITE: [*feebly*] Help me...

>*The unidentified* MAN *moves to another folder.* WHITE *drags himself forward. A sudden tinkling of the wind bell as a gust moves it.*

Help... help...

>*The unidentified* MAN *takes something from the folder—a sheaf of papers—looks at it briefly, then puts it in his pocket.*

Help...

>*The unidentified* MAN *moves to* WHITE, *and takes a pistol out of his pocket. Quickly and without ceremony he stands over* WHITE, *puts the pistol behind his ear and shoots.* WHITE's *body leaps into the air.*
>
>*Blackout.*
>
>*A phone rings.*

SCENE TWO

Michael Wells' city apartment. Night.

WELLS *and* CAREW *are dressed to go out;* CAREW *is wearing a smart coat. He holds a glass of spirits. The phone stops ringing.*

Lights up firstly on CAREW. *Lights up on* WELLS *in the foreground, standing pensively next to the phone. A slight pause.*

CAREW: What is it?

A slight pause.

WELLS: Graham White's dead.

A slight pause. CAREW *sips from his drink.*

CAREW: It's a nice apartment, Mike. How much did you pay for the Whiteley?

A slight pause. WELLS *goes to pick up the phone.*

WELLS: I'll have to ring the Premier.

CAREW: Why?

WELLS: He'll want to know.

CAREW: No he won't: you're the fixer, aren't you?

A slight pause.

What was it? Suicide? I heard he'd been under a lot of pressure since that land scandal.

WELLS *pulls his hand back;* CAREW *looks at his watch.*

We'd better hurry up: we'll be late for dinner.

WELLS: [*angrily*] What do you think's going to happen if the police start poking around Charlie Palmer's backyard?

CAREW: They won't.

He gulps his drink and picks up a copy of Militant Voice.

Keeping an eye on the left of the Party, I see. [*Reading the headline*] 'Michael Wells Blocks Anti-Corruption Committee'. You'd better watch out for this Allen Fitzgerald character, Michael. He seems to be a bit of a firebrand.

WELLS: He thinks he's still playing university politics.

CAREW: You can learn a lot at university.

WELLS: I don't know, I never went.

CAREW *finishes his drink.*

CAREW: We should go. Andrews is only in town till tomorrow. I don't think he'll like being kept waiting.

WELLS: If he wants to make a deal, he'll wait.

ACT ONE

CAREW: Listen, Mike: TransOcean could buy and sell this state, so don't go in there acting The Godfather. I know you don't like Americans, but just think of all the trouble he's going to save you.

A slight pause.

WELLS: You feel pretty secure, don't you?
CAREW: You've got more to lose than me—that's all.

A slight pause.

WELLS: Where's my coat?
CAREW: Is it always this cold this time of year?
WELLS: No. There's something wrong with the weather.
CAREW: The same in the States—everything's upside down.
WELLS: You can't tell from Australia.

Blackout.

Immediately, the sound of a train in the underground.

SCENE THREE

Seven months later. An underground railway station.

ALLEN, *holding a briefcase, is on his way home.*

This is a transitional scene between Scenes One and Two and the body of the play. It should convey the movement of time, in addition to the sense of Allen's isolation and a perception of general social breakdown.

ALLEN *walks past a series of disturbing vignettes, with the rhythmic sound of a train and a stark, flickering light adding to the atmosphere.*

FIRST IMAGE

A poorly-dressed WOMAN *with a baby; a* DRUNK *on the ground.*
A VOICE *sings: 'Zip-a-Dee-Doo-Dah'.*

SECOND IMAGE

A punk GIRL *and* BOY *go through the pockets of a bashed* MAN.
She says: 'Fuckin' hurry up'.

THIRD IMAGE

A DERELICT *with the DTs. He calls out: 'Come on—where are ya? Come on!'*

FOURTH IMAGE

> *A drunk* EVANGELIST: *'And the Lord saith: "I am the Light and the Truth and the Way and whosoever follows me shall gain eternal life and he who spurns me..."'*

FIFTH IMAGE

> *A* FATHER *looking for a lost child. He cries, distraught:* 'Lisa! Lisa! Has anyone seen a little girl. Can't anyone help me?... Lisa!'
>
> *A* MAN *in a tunnel cries:* 'Heaven!'

SIXTH IMAGE

> *A* BUSKER *sings Bob Dylan's 'Baby Blue'.*
>
> *A* WOMAN *screams in the distance.*

SEVENTH IMAGE

> LOUISE *is drinking alone (as in the next scene).*
>
> *The sound of the train increases. The lights change; we hear the train stop.*

SCENE FOUR

Allen and Louise's house. Night.

ALLEN *is cutting carrots on the kitchen table. A bottle of wine is standing on the floor.* LOUISE, *holding a glass of wine, moves behind him continually.*

ALLEN *has come home unexpectedly, half expecting to find* LOUISE *and* JANE *in bed. This is the subtext of the scene, and the major source of the tension. The central difficulty, as will become apparent, is that the agreement between* ALLEN *and* LOUISE *concerning sexuality, based on an understanding of capitalism and the family, prevents either from expressing clearly their anxiety and jealousy.*

LOUISE: I just wasn't expecting you home.
ALLEN: I thought you were going out.
LOUISE: I didn't.
ALLEN: So why are you wandering around worrying about a play you saw a month ago?

LOUISE: It's just those Kafkaesque characters full of neurotic guilt—
ALLEN: There's nothing neurotic about Kafka's characters.
LOUISE: Why do you contradict me all the time?
ALLEN: You're wrong.
LOUISE: Are normal people frightened of turning into cockroaches?
ALLEN: I'm absolutely certain I'm turning into a cockroach.
LOUISE: I said 'normal' people, Allen.
ALLEN: 'Normal' people feel guilt and fear punishment. It's psychopaths like Nixon and Kissinger—
LOUISE: About what? What do normal people feel guilty about?
ALLEN: You're the Jew. You tell me.
LOUISE: I see: you married me so you could plug into four thousand years of neurotic guilt— Catholicism not mad enough for you, Allen?
ALLEN: Oh, for Chrissake: I didn't even see the play.
LOUISE: Listen, any schmuck can get up on a stage and say, 'Why are we here?' or, 'To be or not to be', and make the audience feel like they've had a religious experience for fifteen bucks: all I'm saying is it's bullshit!
ALLEN: So much for Western Civilisation.
LOUISE: People's anxieties have more concrete causes than the fact that those people exist: nuclear war, Allen, inflation, unemployment.
ALLEN: Sure. But they do exist, and they do feel guilty!
LOUISE: Why?
ALLEN: There's hunger in this country! There's suffering! I didn't cause that, but it makes me feel guilty. Is that neurotic?
LOUISE: Yes it is. It should make you feel angry; not guilty. What use is feeling guilty about it?
ALLEN: I didn't realise we were talking about the utility of emotions.
LOUISE: You're talking about capitalism, Allen: there's something we can do about capitalism. There's absolutely nothing we can do about existential guilt.
ALLEN: Yes, we're trapped.
LOUISE: Why should I negotiate with the bourgeoisie about their despair? If they feel so fucking empty and meaningless why don't they just piss off? The rent's due.
ALLEN: Pass the poison.
LOUISE: What are you doing?

ALLEN: I'm preparing my dinner which my wife, caught up in her deliberations about who's guilty and who isn't, neglected to prepare.
LOUISE: I thought you were eating at your parents'.
ALLEN: I didn't.
LOUISE: Well, why blame me?
ALLEN: Do you always get drunk when you're not expecting me home?
LOUISE: Why is it that when a woman drinks alone, she's a drunk; but when a man drinks alone, he's thoughtful?
ALLEN: I don't know, Mister Bones, why is it—?
LOUISE: I'm not drunk.
ALLEN: That's a pity—I thought it might have been a touching sign of affection.
LOUISE: I saw a rug we could— You didn't have to say that.
ALLEN: Say what?
LOUISE: You don't listen to me, do you? You just throw out these one-liners whenever there's a silence.

Pause.

I saw a rug we could put in here.
ALLEN: What's wrong with that one?
LOUISE: It was ruined when you left the doors open in the storm!
ALLEN: It looks alright to me.
LOUISE: Alright, I'll put it in your kennel. Don't you care what the house looks like?
ALLEN: If all you want to talk about is the fucking rug!
LOUISE: [*after a slight pause*] What? Why didn't you eat at your parents'?
ALLEN: Why? Did I disturb—?
LOUISE: No! You didn't. Were you able to talk to our man the Minister?
ALLEN: He told me what I told you: there's no money.
LOUISE: There's fucking money, alright. When he's off every month with his international junkets.
ALLEN: You got your budget.
LOUISE: You're the Auditor General now, are you?
ALLEN: You're not the only bloody women's refuge in the state.
LOUISE: Not yet. Maybe next year, eh? If we're good girls. Why are you defending him? Because he's supposed to be a leftist!
ALLEN: I didn't come home to be interrogated.

ACT ONE

LOUISE: Is everything that happens in that party so secret you can't even talk about it without getting paranoid?
ALLEN: What are you trying to say?
LOUISE: What did you mean, did you disturb me?

A slight pause.

Hey? You could say, 'I'm sorry'.

Pause.

No, not Allen Fitzgerald! Not the best economist in the country; not the leader of the Militant Left faction!

A slight pause.

ALLEN: What did you think I meant?
LOUISE: Why didn't you eat at your parents'?
ALLEN: What's it matter whether I ate there or not?
LOUISE: Don't pretend, Allen, that I'm the one being irrational.
ALLEN: I don't know what you're talking about.
LOUISE: You're doing this on purpose!

Pause.

Why didn't you?
ALLEN: Because I didn't want to sit there for the nth time with them asking me, 'How's Louise? Is everything alright? Will you be coming up for Easter?'

A slight pause.

LOUISE: I wish we had interesting conversations like that. Tell them.
ALLEN: Tell them what?
LOUISE: Easter! What do they want to do? Have a family pogrom! Tell them what I've told them a hundred times: I like them—
ALLEN: You 'like' them.
LOUISE: What am I supposed to do, adore them?
ALLEN: What are they? Neighbours?
LOUISE: Okay, I'll hate them if that makes it sound more intimate. I don't know them, Allen.
ALLEN: Six years we've been married and you don't know my parents?
LOUISE: I married you, not your parents! This is ridiculous...
ALLEN: They're old people! They've got the right to some happiness.

LOUISE: I'm the Jew, Allen: I'm the one who's supposed to be running around serving chicken soup and worrying about the family. They can come here; we can go to a restaurant—
ALLEN: They want you to eat with them!
LOUISE: No! Not in the castle of patriarchy with your mother beetling around under huge platters of meat and your father acting like he just opened the Red Sea!
ALLEN: That's their home!
LOUISE: Well, it's not mine and I don't like it.

A slight pause.

ALLEN: I don't—
LOUISE: All I want is to be treated like I actually exist!
ALLEN: What's wrong with the way they treat you?
LOUISE: They treat me like your wife!
ALLEN: Will you stop mouthing off like a feminist primer—?
LOUISE: 'A feminist primer', Allen? What's that?
ALLEN: I want you to respect my parents!
LOUISE: When they stop treating me like the heathen who trapped their famous son.
ALLEN: That's bullshit!
LOUISE: I know it is. I told your mother: 'If he was famous, he'd have a Nobel Prize'.
ALLEN: Don't you believe you've got any obligations to them?
LOUISE: This is— What obligations? You want me to wash their car?
ALLEN: To honour them in their home. Can't you take anything seriously?
LOUISE: I'm trying under extreme provocation to remain human.

Pause.

ALLEN: You hurt your parents, you hurt mine—
LOUISE: How many carrots are you going to eat?
ALLEN: I'm going to eat them all! I'm going to eat every last fucking one!
LOUISE: Don't be so Freudian.
ALLEN: [*picking up a carrot*] Here! I'm eating my cock! That's what you're doing to me!
LOUISE: I know what you're trying to do, Allen.
ALLEN: I'm trying to have a reasonable discussion—

ACT ONE

LOUISE: What do you think the feminist analysis of the family's about?
ALLEN: I don't know what it's about. Causing as much unhappiness—
LOUISE: Why do you think—?
ALLEN: Destroying any basis for personal support!
LOUISE: Will you shut up and listen to me? Why do you think I spend my time trying to sort out the problems of battered wives—
ALLEN: You're a masochist.
LOUISE: —with biblical motorheads bashing at the door bellowing for 'their' women and 'their' children?!
ALLEN: That's not me!
LOUISE: Don't shake that fucking knife at me!
ALLEN: How is turning us into personal atoms occasionally bumping into one another for sexual union a leap forward in human happiness?
LOUISE: So in the interests of human happiness I'm supposed to have your dinner ready when I'm not expecting you home.
ALLEN: I was joking about that.
LOUISE: I'm sorry, I'm just a humourless feminist.
ALLEN: All I want is some peace when I get home.
LOUISE: Why? If you can't yell at people you love, who can you yell at?
ALLEN: Do you know what Wells is saying about me? Do you know what I heard today? That I'm a fucking KGB agent.
LOUISE: At least then we could afford an overseas holiday.
ALLEN: Don't you know what that means?
LOUISE: You're not taking it seriously, are you?
ALLEN: Of course I'm taking it seriously. He could have me named before the commission!
LOUISE: He could have Mickey Mouse named, too. Maybe we should get rid of our ears before the cops arrive.
ALLEN: Do you have any affection left for me, Louise?
LOUISE: I love you! Can't you get it through your thick head? If that's the sort of garbage you have to put up with, why don't you get out of the stinking party?
ALLEN: Why did we get married?
LOUISE: We got married because of our parents, remember?

A slight pause.

ALLEN: If that was the only reason, we were wrong.

LOUISE: [*crying*] Why do you do this to me? I love you, fuck it! Do you want me to say it again? I love you! I love you! When the whole world's against you, I love you! But I can't give you everything. I've got to save a little bit for myself.
ALLEN: What am I asking that's so impossible?
LOUISE: You want my will!

The lights change. Birds screech.

SCENE FIVE

A bourgeois party. Night. The action is divided into three sequences.

FIRST SEQUENCE

A balcony overlooking the harbour.

ALLEN, *dressed as before, is standing thoughtfully and unaware of* ROSE, *a little way behind him.* ALLEN *has a copy of George Gilder's* Wealth and Poverty *by his side.* ROSE *is extremely attractive. Pause.*

ROSE: It's beautiful, isn't it?
ALLEN: [*startled*] What? The harbour?
ROSE: The wind bell.

A slight pause.

ALLEN: Yes, it is.
ROSE: [*stepping forward*] I'm Rose Draper.
ALLEN: Oh— G'day— [*Putting out his hand*] I'm Allen Fitzgerald.
ROSE: [*shaking hands*] I know.
ALLEN: [*amused*] You do, eh? What are you? A cop?
ROSE: I'm a journalist.
ALLEN: Oh— Rose Draper! Right. You work for *Business Review*—Yeah. I've read some of your stuff.
ROSE: What did you think?
ALLEN: Good. That last piece you did on the oil industry was terrific.
ROSE: I used some of your research in it.
ALLEN: Yes.
ROSE: I tried to acknowledge you in the article but the editor cut it out.
ALLEN: That's what editors are for. How is old rumbleguts?

ACT ONE

ROSE: You know him?
ALLEN: Sure. We went to university together. We were both anarchists at the same time— I thought he might be here tonight.
ROSE: He was invited to Canberra by the Prime Minister.
ALLEN: Two great economic minds meet. Does he still tell the plastic bag baby joke?
ROSE: Yes.
ALLEN: Yeah, the thing about conservatives is they have such a bad sense of humour.
ROSE: Anyone who thought up the Liberal Party couldn't be totally humourless.
ALLEN: So how come *Business Review*'s publishing attacks on multinationals now?
ROSE: I wasn't attacking multinationals—I was reporting the facts.
ALLEN: I've been reporting the facts for five years and all I've got is an ASIO file.
ROSE: You must have let a few value judgements slip in.
ALLEN: No. That piece you did was really good—it must have been hard to get some of those figures.
ROSE: No.
ALLEN: Production costs? Internal pricing? None of that's on public record.
ROSE: You can find out anything if you want.

The music is turned up suddenly: Blondie's 'Hanging on the Telephone'. JANICE *enters.*

JANICE: [*to* ROSE] Oh—you found him! [*To* ALLEN] I didn't know where you'd gotten to, Allen. What are you doing out here? I'm sure Rose is cold. That's a lovely dress! Pity Louise couldn't come: I hope she feels better tomorrow.
ALLEN: I'm sorry, Janice, Louise isn't sick—she just doesn't get on with Bob.
JANICE: [*carefully, without rancour*] Why did you say that, Allen? For my benefit or yours?

The lights change. The music volume increases.

SECOND SEQUENCE

The lounge room. Guests are standing, talking.

BOB *strides across the room toward the emerging* ALLEN *et al. He is carrying a glass and a bottle of red wine. A* MAN *calls, above the music.*

MAN: Happy birthday!

BOB: Thanks! Where's my present?

WOMAN: They're terrific! The Liberals couldn't do any better!

The song has reached the chorus. BOB *sings his own variation loudly.*

BOB: [*singing, looking at* ROSE]
    'Oh! Why can't we fuck again?
    Oh! Why can't we fuck again?'

JANICE: Here's the man himself.

BOB *comes up and embraces* JANICE *from behind.*

BOB: How's my delectable wife and her equally scrumptious companions—except him.

JANICE: [*to* BOB] Don't do that.

BOB: [*to* ALLEN] You don't look your normal rabid self, mate—what happened? [*Referring to* ROSE] She knock you back?

ALLEN: [*animatedly*] 'Nobody says no to the king!'

BOB: [*singing*] 'Tooty frooty, I want a rooty!'

ALLEN *joins in.*

ALLEN & BOB: [*singing together*]
    'Tooty frooty, I want a rooty!
    'Tooty frooty, I want a rooty!
    'Ah wop bapa boolop, a wam bam boom!'

JANICE: [*to* ROSE] It's a rite they go through whenever they meet. Much like dogs sniffing.

BOB: We're not appreciated around here, mate. Where's your glass?

ALLEN: I don't— [have one.]

BOB: [*pouring wine into a glass*] Have mine—

JANICE: [*trying to look at the bottle*] What's that?

BOB: I seem to remember that jacket—summer of sixty-eight, wasn't it?

JANICE: [*having seen the label*] Oh—what nice person gave you that?

BOB: [*to* ROSE] He believes in wearing his heart on his sleeve.

ALLEN: That's not my heart, it's my lunch. [*Holding up the book*] Hey, what are you reading this Gilder shit for?

ACT ONE

BOB: [*pouring wine into* ROSE*'s glass*] I knew you'd find it, you red bastard! Did you read the bit about capitalism?

JANICE: I don't have a glass, Bob.

BOB: [*ignoring her*] I'm going to have it inscribed and hung over my desk: 'Capitalism begins with giving'.

ALLEN: [*offering his glass to* JANICE] Here, have this, Janice—

BOB: No! Drink up! The most expensive piss you're ever likely to see—

JANICE: I don't have a glass, Bob.

BOB: Then get one!

    JANICE *promptly moves off.*

She hasn't heard of women's liberation. But, I mean, it's so fucking wonderful: 'Under capitalism, the ventures of reason are launched into a world ruled by morality and providence'. It's like Adam Smith in drag! Fantastic! No wonder the Yankee economy's fucked!

ROSE: Why are you reading it?

BOB: It's required reading at the bank: you can't have a piss without some fuckhead telling you we've got to sell the Post Office to Kerry Packer. And talking of dubious scenario situations, I'm trying to get Miss Investigative Journalist here to do an exposé on the bank—you know how much they lost on foreign exchange transactions last year? [*Pointing*] There's the moron over there—he's been transferred over to Reserve, thank Christ. God help our balance of payments next year.

    The MAN *being pointed at waves.*

[*Calling*] Having a good time? [*To* ALLEN *and* ROSE] And you ask why the economy's in such a mess. [*To* ALLEN] How are things down at the Provisional Revolutionary Government? The collective decided what kind of toilet paper is ecologically sound, yet?

ALLEN: Everything's set for Tuesday.

BOB: Tuesday, eh? Well, I hope it doesn't interfere with my golf game. Reckon you could keep the fighting away from Southlakes for the afternoon?

ALLEN: Since when did you take up golf?

BOB: Since I figured out brownnosing was the only way you got anywhere in this country. What are the fringe benefits with the insurgent masses like nowadays?

ALLEN: We just took a wage cut.
BOB: It's good to see the workers' vanguard setting a responsible example. At least revolutionaries get more fucks.
ROSE: You've got a funny idea about what women find attractive.
BOB: Have you heard the one about the feminist who married the football player?
ROSE: No.
BOB: What's the joke? [*To* ALLEN] So what are you so down in the mouth about? The recession not going the way you hoped?
ALLEN: You know what I saw coming over here? You know how cold it is—there's a woman in a cotton dress with a suitcase pushing a pram up and down in front of a telephone box. Eight-thirty at night.
BOB: Well, did you stop and do the Christian thing? Offer her a nutritious meal in a modest but warm abode?

   A slight pause.

Where's that woman? Am I going to get the ice treatment now? Michael Wells is here—have you seen him yet?
ALLEN: Wells! What'd you invite him for?
BOB: I was looking for a good fight—don't disappoint me.

   He sees JANICE *returning with a glass.*

[*To* ROSE] So what are you working on? Or should I rather say, 'Who'?
ROSE: Here she comes.
ALLEN: You're so fucking cynical...
BOB: [*aggressively*] What?
JANICE: [*holding her glass to* BOB] Bob, cynical? He's just got a guilty conscience. Thanks, Bob.

   A slight pause.

ALLEN: What's so special about the wine?
JANICE: Chateau Mouton Rothschild.
BOB: Two hundred dollars a bottle—and that was before devaluation.
JANICE: [*drinking*] What's it like?
BOB: Sheep dip—that's the *'mouton'* part. What am I cynical about?
ALLEN: Everything. Look at this shit, Bob. That woman's out there pushing her pram around in the cold and we're up here drinking two-hundred-dollar bottles of wine and making fun of the profession

ACT ONE

we're both making a living from. If you don't think that's cynical, what is it?

BOB: Realism, mate. Nobody ever got paid for telling the truth.

ALLEN: If people had the truth maybe they could do something about it.

BOB: If they had the truth maybe they'd kill themselves.

JANICE: The difference between you and Bob, Allen, is that Bob doesn't believe in anything anymore.

ALLEN: I'd like to see that at the end of one of the bank's economic forecasts.

JANICE: What's your analysis of the present recession, Allen?

BOB: It's the end of capitalism.

JANICE: [*to* ALLEN] Do you think it's the end of capitalism?

BOB: [*turning to leave*] If you're going to get heavy, I think I'll go and molest a few twelve-year-olds. I don't seem to be having much luck here.

JANICE: You haven't asked me yet, dear.

BOB: I was saving you as a last resort.

JANICE: I thought that was all you had left.

BOB: She's very witty, my wife, isn't she? It's a pity she didn't follow her father into the Supreme Court.

JANICE: It wouldn't have been nearly as much fun as following you into the morass.

BOB: I'll be Chief Economist in five years, Allen.

ALLEN: You'll probably be sold off to the Bank of America by then.

BOB: I don't care who I work for—I'd even work for you if you promised me a *dacha* on the Black Sea.

ALLEN: Give us a call after the revolution.

BOB: I don't think so. I think I'll be on the first Hercules out after the Yanks have bombed the shit out of the joint.

Pause. The Rolling Stones are heard, singing 'Satisfaction'.

ALLEN: I hope you're happy

BOB: Who's happy? They're playing our song, dear. [*Drinking from the bottle*] To nihilism!

He wanders off. A slight pause.

JANICE: Do all men react so badly to turning forty, Allen?

ALLEN: When we were at school and uni, I used to think he was joking.

JANICE: He is. We all are, finally, aren't we? Don't be depressed if you can't understand him: we all have our limitations. Oh, look, there's your friend Cathy Stevens. I must go and say hello.

    JANICE *exits. A slight pause.*

ALLEN: Everything stays unsaid.
ROSE: You're not listening closely enough. Why did you come tonight?
ALLEN: I was about to ask the same question.
ROSE: Why?
ALLEN: Aren't you and Bob fucking?
ROSE: No. He asked me, but we're not.
ALLEN: Janice thinks you are.
ROSE: Probably.
ALLEN: So you accepted Bob's invitation knowing his wife probably thought you were fucking as a way of keeping the adrenalin going.
ROSE: No, as a way of meeting you.
ALLEN: That's flattering.
ROSE: I'm glad you think so.
ALLEN: Why? Is there an ulterior motive?
ROSE: There always is.
ALLEN: So what is it?
ROSE: That wouldn't be keeping secrets, would it?
ALLEN: No, but it might clarify things.
ROSE: No it wouldn't.
ALLEN: Tell me you're working for the CIA.
ROSE: Alright, I am.
ALLEN: And your mission is to terminate me.
ROSE: Yes. How long will it be before you frighten yourself?
ALLEN: Make a suggestion.
ROSE: That I'll destroy your soul.
ALLEN: It sounds more interesting every minute.
ROSE: You're such an innocent.
ALLEN: Do I pay for this by the half-hour, or what?
ROSE: I've read most of what you've written: it's very impressive. Michael Wells is standing behind you and he's been looking at us every five minutes for the last half hour. I think you'd better go and talk to him.

ACT ONE

ALLEN: You mean you don't want to lose your government sources by being seen talking to me.
ROSE: You're married, aren't you?
ALLEN: Yes.
ROSE: You don't blink—I like that.
ALLEN: How old do you think you are?
ROSE: I'm as old as sin.
ALLEN: Is that supposed to frighten me?
ROSE: Why did you come tonight?
ALLEN: My friends invited me.
ROSE: They're not your friends. [*Moving off*] Tell me when you're leaving.

> *All sound effects stop.* ALLEN *wanders across to where* WELLS *is standing with two* MEN.

FIRST MAN: All we need is a three per cent swing against us and we've lost the seat.
SECOND MAN: It's a marginal seat we expected to lose.
WELLS: We won't lose it. [*Seeing* ALLEN] Well, Allen. Fancy meeting you here.
ALLEN: My thoughts exactly, Mike.
WELLS: I'd have thought it wouldn't be proletarian enough for you.
ALLEN: What are you doing here?
WELLS: Bob's been doing some work for us. I saw Cathy Stevens here a little earlier— Are you and she…?
ALLEN: I thought you tried to keep up with things, Mike.
WELLS: I do, I do. I noticed you having a little *tête à tête* with Rose Draper over there. Telling her all our secrets, were you?
ALLEN: We don't have any secrets, Mike: we're a democratic socialist party.
WELLS: You like saying it, don't you, Allen? So how do you think the government's going? Do you think we'll win the by-election?
ALLEN: We'll lose.
WELLS: I guess that'd give you a certain private satisfaction.
ALLEN: The candidate stinks.
WELLS: Just because Red Ted didn't get preselected is no reason to get abusive.

ALLEN: He's a real estate agent. Everyone in the electorate knows he's up to his neck in council corruption.
WELLS: Is that so?
ALLEN: If we lose that election, Mike, it'll be your fault.
WELLS: And what if we win?
ALLEN: It'll be just dumb luck.
WELLS: There's a real problem here for people like you, isn't there, Allen? The people you regard as totally corrupt and incompetent keep winning the elections, while the faultless voice of reason and morality keeps forfeiting its money to the Electoral Office. What's your theory on that?
ALLEN: What's yours?
WELLS: I'm quite happy to say the voters are as thick as bricks, but I don't think that'd rest well on your mantle.
ALLEN: Do you know how many unemployed there are in the country now, Mike? How much industry is being destroyed? How many homeless there are? Do you know what the suicide rate is?
WELLS: My secretary tries to keep me up with things.
ALLEN: Well, what the fuck are you doing about it?
WELLS: We're trying to deal with it.
ALLEN: How? By putting real estate agents in parliament?
WELLS: We can get real estate agents in, mate! We'd be pushing shit uphill trying to get anyone in under the slogan of 'Workers' Power'. Why do my tactics work and yours don't?
ALLEN: You don't have any tactics! You blow whatever way the morning editorials push you.
WELLS: We're still in power.
ALLEN: And as soon as you've saved the country for the ruling class you'll be back on your ears in the opposition.
WELLS: With a legacy of legislative and welfare reforms we'd—
ALLEN: What fucking reforms? A flotilla of royal commissions and inquiries. That'll be our legacy.
WELLS: It might not even be that, comrade, if you split the party and bring down the government.
ALLEN: I'm not splitting the party, Mike. I'm not hand in glove with Charlie Palmer and the Petersville Council putting high-rise developers and racketeers in office—

WELLS: I'd watch what I was saying, buddy-boy: defamation can be extremely expensive.
ALLEN: Have you ever wondered why criminals are your only natural allies, Mike?

Pause.

WELLS: I've seen passion before, but never wrapped up so closely with sheer stupidity.
ALLEN: I'm going to get rid of you, Wells: you and all your whole corrupt gang.
WELLS: Are you? How are you going to do that?
ALLEN: By getting the only thing you respect: the numbers.
WELLS: Easier said than done, Allen. What time is it?
FIRST MAN: Nearly eleven.
WELLS: Pity you missed the late news; you might have heard something interesting.
ALLEN: What?
WELLS: While you've been cavorting away with the bourgeoisie here, the Rules Committee has called in your books. Seems that some of your boys have been stacking the branches.

ALLEN *turns quickly to leave.*

And Allen—

ALLEN *hesitates.*

There's something else to stick in your pipe: an administrator's been appointed to Petersville Council. Maybe you and Charlie Palmer could get together to bring a bit of principled action back into the party.

ALLEN *leaves. A slight pause.*

FIRST MAN: He's finished.

A slight pause.

WELLS: No-one's ever finished till they've got six foot of dirt and a high-rise apartment block on top of them.

The lights change.

THIRD SEQUENCE

A room.

ALLEN *is on the phone.*

ALLEN: Which branches, Ramon?... Jesus. Their books are okay, aren't they? He almost got expelled for doing that the last time!... Well, why didn't you ring my home number? Louise knew where— [*Looking at his watch*] How many times did you ring?... I don't know where she is... Yeah, I'll come in now—you're going to be there, aren't you?...

We see ROSE *approach.*

No, Ramon—I'm coming straight in. *Ciao.*

ALLEN disconnects with his fingers. He lowers the handset, then raises it and begins dialling. He pauses midway and hangs up.

ROSE: Haven't you been expecting this?
ALLEN: Expecting what?
ROSE: A purge.
ALLEN: We were almost there.
ROSE: Only in your dreams.
ALLEN: What do you know about it?

A thunder clap. It begins to rain outside.

ROSE: [*shaking her hair*] At last—enough to know you were fucked when you started.
ALLEN: We're not beaten yet.
ROSE: You've been beaten for forty years.
ALLEN: That's more like the *Business Review* we've come to know and love.
ROSE: That's postwar Australian history.
ALLEN: I'm leaving now.
ROSE: I'll come with you.

The lights change. The sound of rain increases, then fades.

SCENE SIX

The Rank and File Co-ordinating Centre. Night.

ALLEN *and* RAMON *enter brusquely.*

It is obvious that the new developments are a shock to ALLEN, *although he knows clearly what has to be done.*

ACT ONE 21

RAMON: Parklea, Blackberry Hill and Morsetown. They called the branch secretaries in at eight-thirty—where have you been? I was trying to get you everywhere!

A slight pause.

ALLEN: What happened to Russell?
RAMON: I told you—!
ALLEN: Then tell me again!
RAMON: He was bashed.
ALLEN: Why didn't you tell me on the phone? Who was it?
RAMON: Who do you think? Don't be an imbecile. We knew this was going to happen. If all we get out of this are a few bashings, we'll be very lucky. Fascists!
ALLEN: How was the town hall meeting?
RAMON: Good. Maybe a hundred and fifty steelworkers. They passed a resolution condemning the leadership and calling for action to fight further retrenchments.
ALLEN: Anyone from my father's plant?
RAMON: No. Idiots.

A slight pause.

Where's your wife?
ALLEN: I don't know!

Pause.

RAMON: We are going to win this steelworkers' election, mate; but it won't mean nothing if all our branch delegates on the executive are expelled.

A slight pause.

ALLEN: A hundred and fifty.
RAMON: Yes! A hundred and fifty! There were none when I started.
ALLEN: It's a drop in the ocean!
RAMON: You stick to the branches. That's what you know. We need one more big factory: Austeel. What's wrong with those bastards? They had seventy men put off last week and not one delegate came to our meeting!

A slight pause.

ALLEN: Are you asking me?
RAMON: Sure—your father works there.
ALLEN: My brother was killed in Vietnam! Why do you think he's anti-communist?
RAMON: It'd be a better reason to be anti-imperialist!
ALLEN: Haven't you ever noticed the way people's eyes glaze over when you use a word like 'imperialism'?
RAMON: What words are we supposed to use: 'American Peacekeeping Forces'?
ALLEN: You talk to people in words they understand.
RAMON: They don't understand anything. All they are interested in is sport and drinking.
ALLEN: That's where—
RAMON: Who broke them? How did this happen to this people?
ALLEN: My father's a reactionary Catholic bastard.
RAMON: He's a worker having his throat cut!
ALLEN: He doesn't even recognise himself as a worker!

Pause.

RAMON: There's something sick in the soul of this country.

A slight pause.

ALLEN: If we could block the investigation to the branches till after the steelworkers' election, we'd have the numbers on the executive to overturn the ruling.

Pause.

RAMON: You know what we have to do, don't you?
ALLEN: What?
RAMON: Charlie Palmer—
ALLEN: No!
RAMON: Yes, Allen. You listen to me. Charlie Palmer is the seventh man on the rules committee. He holds the balance.
ALLEN: We've been trying to get rid of him for three years!
RAMON: We have to do a deal!
ALLEN: No!
RAMON: You tell me how else we can hold up proceedings.
ALLEN: He's a criminal, Ramon. What sort of credibility—by what right could we claim to represent an alternative—?

RAMON: If we don't do it, we'll be back where we were three years ago.
ALLEN: If we do we might as well have never started.
RAMON: That's exactly the way I feel. I should never have wasted my time in this bullshit bourgeois party!

A slight pause.

ALLEN: There's such a thing as principle.
RAMON: And there's such things as ballot stuffing, branch stacking and the bashing of leftists!
ALLEN: We've built up our support by opposition to those sort of tactics!
RAMON: We built up our support because our aims are right!
ALLEN: And what'll happen to that support when we start getting into bed with Charlie Palmer?
RAMON: They'll say we didn't make this world and we didn't put these criminals in charge.
ALLEN: They'll say we're no better than them.
RAMON: If they're so politically fucked they can't see the importance of compromising now so we can win later.
ALLEN: How many compromises later?

Pause.

RAMON: *Atonico! Absolutemente atonico!*

A slight pause.

ALLEN: We can't, in our personal behaviour, subvert the values we want in a socialist—
RAMON: Shut up! You don't know what you're talking about.

A slight pause.

What do you think I am? The devil? This isn't heaven, mate, and it's not hell: this is the world— Are you listening to me?
ALLEN: I'm trying to think!
RAMON: Are we going to win power by our good deeds?
ALLEN: We're not fighting for power. We're fighting for a society where people can live with some kind of dignity and security.
RAMON: We need three weeks! Just three weeks. And then we'll have that fucking union and we'll have the executive.
ALLEN: Wells taunted me by saying we should make a deal with Palmer.
RAMON: Because he thinks you're such a baby you'd rather commit political suicide than face up to your responsibilities.

ALLEN: Why has Wells moved against Palmer? Why would he move against his own power base? That's the key, isn't it, Ramon?

RAMON: I don't know why.

ALLEN: Well, instead of acting like a fucking bull in a china shop, why not try and think why?

RAMON: The thing I think, my friend, is this is our only hope and Wells doesn't think we're smart enough to take it.

ALLEN: We'll be discredited.

RAMON: Was Lenin discredited because he accepted help from German warmongers?

ALLEN: How can you compare that with our situation?

RAMON: I don't know what you think we're doing, Allen, but let me tell you. When I say we are going to have socialism in this country, I mean it.

ALLEN: And at the heart of socialism is the idea of justice, and if we betray that, we betray everything, even if we achieve power.

RAMON: They bash our delegates! They spend a quarter of a million dollars on the election campaign! They hold onto their power like dead men! We must be hard, like them. Otherwise we're fucked.

ALLEN: No, Ramon!

RAMON: I'm not asking you, I'm telling you: if you don't do this, the betrayal of our hopes and work is on your head.

ALLEN: Can't you hear what you're saying?

The lights change. All sound effects stop. There is a muffled sound of engines, as on a ship.

SCENE SEVEN

Allen and Louise's house. Night.

ALLEN *makes moves on the computer chess set. There is a sound of papers being fluttered by the wind. He returns to a folio of papers and completes a calculation on a calculator: the slightest hint of mania. The papers stop fluttering.*

LOUISE *enters. The engine room noise fades.*

LOUISE: Why are you up so late?

A slight pause.

ACT ONE 25

ALLEN: I didn't hear you come in.
>*Pause.* LOUISE *takes off her coat and moves toward the door.*

LOUISE: What are you doing?
>*The computer chess signals it is ready to move.*

ALLEN: The transformation problem— Don't close the doors.
LOUISE: It's cold.
ALLEN: I'm not.
>*A slight pause.*

LOUISE: You haven't done anything on that since you left uni.
>*Pause.*

The transformation problem and computer chess—what's wrong?
ALLEN: Nothing.
LOUISE: How was Bob's party?
ALLEN: What you'd expect.
LOUISE: You're a terrific conversationalist.
>*A slight pause.*

Do you want to be left alone?
ALLEN: No.
LOUISE: It's stopped raining.
>*A slight pause.*

I hate it after a storm—the leaves, the smells—like a graveyard. Decay.
ALLEN: Where were you?
LOUISE: Out.
ALLEN: With her?
LOUISE: No... I was thinking about... We always seem so certain when we talk about the past—the causes of the First World War; the relationship between class forces—why do we feel so helpless in trying to understand the present?
>*A slight pause.*

ALLEN: The complexity of the factors involved— Who could have predicted the events since the election? The particular interaction of personality and politics?
LOUISE: What's wrong?

ALLEN: [*upset*] I find it so hard—the cruelty—the brutality... You stand in a group of people, and you feel like screaming, 'How? How can you be like this?'

A slight pause.

LOUISE: Why did you go?

Pause.

Allen?

ALLEN: I hate my weakness.
LOUISE: You're not weak.
ALLEN: I was worried about you.
LOUISE: I didn't know what time you'd be home.
ALLEN: You didn't tell me you were going out.
LOUISE: I didn't want to stay in the house by myself.
ALLEN: Ramon tried to ring and couldn't get hold of me.
LOUISE: Why are you attacking me?

Pause.

ALLEN: I was worried about you.

A slight pause.

How can you do this to me?
LOUISE: Please, Allen...
ALLEN: How? Do you think I'm a fool?
LOUISE: I won't fight with you, Allen. Not every night.
ALLEN: Then why do you see her? How can you sleep with her? I'm your husband!
LOUISE: Does that give you the right to tell me what I can and can't do?
ALLEN: Even if we weren't married I couldn't tolerate it!
LOUISE: But I can tolerate you and Cathy Stevens sleeping in my bed.

Pause.

ALLEN: Is this your revenge?
LOUISE: No, it's not! I just want to be granted the freedom you granted yourself!

A slight pause.

ALLEN: I told you. You knew. We agreed.
LOUISE: Yes, we agreed.

ALLEN: Why do you want me to feel guilty?
LOUISE: I don't! I want you to see that guilt for what it is! Can't you see I'm like you? I fear! I cry!
ALLEN: Can you hear the engines?
LOUISE: What engines?
ALLEN: Of the machines turning. Every cog turning.
LOUISE: We're not prisoners!
ALLEN: What are we? Two people who love each other who spend all their time tearing each other apart!
LOUISE: Do we have to?
ALLEN: What do you want of me?
LOUISE: You don't mean that! If only you did, but you don't.
ALLEN: What can I do? I'm sorry. I didn't mean to hurt you.
LOUISE: You did and you want me to judge you.
ALLEN: I want peace!
LOUISE: Everything is directed to you. Your needs, your fear, your trial. It's like nobody else exists.
ALLEN: Why do you love me?
LOUISE: Do you want me to say I don't!
ALLEN: If that's what you think—
LOUISE: I don't know anymore! You stand in the ring and you crack your whip— Why, Allen? What's it all about?
ALLEN: Are you so blind you can't see what you're doing?
LOUISE: I'm trying to live my life!
ALLEN: Doesn't that involve me?
LOUISE: You argue on my ground for once! Why can't you be happy? Why can't you look through the doors and see the garden?

A slight pause.

ALLEN: You don't know what I'm talking about, do you?
LOUISE: Stop trying to will everything!
ALLEN: You're the one so insecure you think everything's an attack on your will.
LOUISE: Insecurity? Is that why you want to be a husband?
ALLEN: I work with her, Louise! We work together. We oppose one another politically. I see her every day! How am I supposed to put up with it?
LOUISE: Just stop thinking of me as your property!

ALLEN: You're my wife!
LOUISE: The engines are inside you. It's your own relentlessness.
ALLEN: I'm trying to hold onto one of the last things left; one of the few remaining fragments of personal happiness.
LOUISE: How do you think I feel at the refuge? It's hard, I'd like support.
ALLEN: All of this because of some crazy theory about marriage and the family.
LOUISE: I know what I want, and I know how I feel…
ALLEN: I don't want my life to be your social laboratory!
LOUISE: You're wrong! You're wrong! There are friends. There are comrades. You're not alone.
ALLEN: I am, Louise. You don't know how alone I am.
LOUISE: [*pathetically*] How could you expect me to stand in the same room as Cathy Stevens?
ALLEN: It's over! I didn't even talk to her.
LOUISE: [*crying*] I can't believe you're the man I fell in love with.
ALLEN: What does love mean to you? What does loyalty? Where are those values in the new lexicon of human relationships?
LOUISE: They're there between people who trust and respect themselves and each other.
ALLEN: In the best of all possible worlds, with sexuality free of obligations, relationships emptied of content and love finally made identical with lust.
LOUISE: I don't know you.
ALLEN: You've convinced me love doesn't exist. It's just the selfish rape of another.
LOUISE: Why can't you ever admit you're wrong?
ALLEN: You're a stranger to me.
LOUISE: Then look at me.

The lights change.

SCENE EIGHT

Wells' office. Day.

WELLS *speaks into an imagined intercom.*

WELLS: Hold the calls for fifteen minutes, Dianne. [*Looking off*] Bob Lang! Come in. It's good to see you.

ACT ONE

BOB: [*entering*] What a terrific view.
WELLS: Better than the Premier's. How's the bank? Keeping you busy?
BOB: They have trouble keeping the paperweights busy.
WELLS: That was a good do at your place the other night.
BOB: You should've stayed for the finale: Janice tipped the punchbowl on me.
WELLS: No, I had a good time. I was surprised to see Allen Fitzgerald there.
BOB: We're old school friends.
WELLS: You see each other much?
BOB: No. Whenever we do we end up fighting.
WELLS: Yeah, he's a bit of a ratbag, isn't he?

> *A very slight pause.*

BOB: He was always round the twist.
WELLS: What makes you say that?
BOB: He's the same now as he was when he was fourteen: still talking revolution, still wanting to storm heaven.
WELLS: What do you think's wrong with him?
BOB: He just never grew up.

> *A slight pause.*

WELLS: I hear you're interested in the job in the Economic Advisory Council?
BOB: Yeah.
WELLS: You wouldn't mind moving to Canberra?
BOB: Not if I was going to do something interesting.

> WELLS *takes out a thick folder.*

WELLS: I'd like you to have a look at something for me.
BOB: Sure.
WELLS: I'll give this to you only on the understanding that it's strictly confidential. There's only two copies, and I've got the other one in my safe. Understood?
BOB: What is it? The blueprint for Vegemite?
WELLS: It's a plan for the reconstruction of the Australian steel industry by TransOcean International.

> *A slight pause.*

BOB: What do you want me to do with it?

WELLS: I want you to go through it and check their figures and see if it's feasible.

A slight pause.

BOB: Why don't you get someone in Treasury to do it?

WELLS: I don't want any leaks, Bob. I don't want you to talk about this to anybody. I just want you to study this document, and then come back to me and tell me if it's possible. How long will it take you?

A slight pause.

BOB: I'd need to get— I haven't done any— How soon do you want it?

WELLS: As soon as possible.

BOB: What—a month? Two months?

WELLS: A fortnight.

A slight pause.

BOB: I'll try.

WELLS: Good. If you need anything, call me. I don't think there'll be any trouble getting you on the job.

A slight pause.

BOB: Okay. Thanks.

WELLS: No-one's to know, Bob, not even your wife.

BOB: That won't be any trouble: we're not talking. They're going to buy out Austeel?

A slight pause.

WELLS: If they've got something that's workable, yes.

The lights change.

SCENE NINE

A building. Night.

ALLEN *is talking to a* THUG.

ALLEN: I'm Allen Fitzgerald... I've got an appointment with Charlie Palmer.

The lights change.

ACT ONE 31

SCENE TEN

The steel mill. Day.

It is as spectacular and terrifying as possible. A MAN *is bashing a chunk of steel with a sledge hammer. There are flames, torches, unbelievable noise.* MEN *are directing a river of molten steel across the floor. An accident is in the process of happening.*

This scene depends entirely upon direction and is open to alteration according to the resources available. Nevertheless, it is the conclusion of the Act and must be directed with this in mind.

BRUCE *runs on stage to perform some function. Without realising, he becomes isolated and is caught amidst the metal.*

BRUCE: The fucking channel's busted!

    Other WORKERS *run on.*

FIRST WORKER: Where is it?
SECOND WORKER: Leave it!
THIRD WORKER: It's broken out! It's coming your way!
DOUG: [*to* BRUCE] Get out of the way!
BRUCE: I can't!
DOUG: Move, for Chrisssake!
FIRST WORKER: Get the crane!
BRUCE: I can't!

    BRUCE *jumps to safety.* DOUG *runs up to him, striking him across the face and embracing him. All sound effects stop.*

DOUG: You want to get killed? You want to fucking get killed!

Blackout.

END OF ACT ONE

ACT TWO

SCENE ONE

Blackout. Lights up.
Wells' office. Day.
WELLS *is at his desk with* SIR LESLIE HARRIS *and* CAREW. HARRIS *is unwrapping a cigar.* DIANNE *enters with a folder. She takes it to* WELLS.

WELLS: The government understands your position, Sir Leslie—
DIANNE: The industry report, Mr Wells.
HARRIS: The company's not interested in your understanding.
WELLS: Thanks, Dianne.

    DIANNE *exits.*

HARRIS: Do you have a cigarette lighter, Mr Carew? I seem to have...
CAREW: I'm sorry, sir, I don't smoke.
HARRIS: [*putting his cigar away*] Well, I know you don't smoke, Wells. I suppose if young Allen Fitzgerald becomes secretary it'll be against the law and you'll have to be in the party to get tobacco.
WELLS: This report shows—
HARRIS: Don't bother me with reports, we've got a library of them.
WELLS: We might be more sympathetic—
HARRIS: I want to know what the government intends to do!

    A slight pause.

WELLS: Until we have a firm commitment from you in the form of concrete plans to restructure your steel division, we don't intend to do anything, Sir Leslie.
HARRIS: So it's basically what you dished up to BHP. No retrenchments in return for bounties and whatnot. Do you think the unions will swallow it once they realise what it means?
WELLS: They don't have any choice.
HARRIS: BHP is one thing. Austeel is another.
WELLS: Smaller.
HARRIS: Smaller, perhaps, but big enough. You see, I'm even more pessimistic than BHP is about the strength of the upturn.

ACT TWO 33

WELLS: I'm sorry to hear that. There aren't too many financial commentators who'd agree.
HARRIS: No, everyone's patting themselves on the back that we avoided disaster by the skin of our teeth last year, and looking forward to a rosy future; but of course there is no rosy future, Michael. We live in a completely different economic environment.
WELLS: Mmm.
HARRIS: The American economy is already overheating; the world debt problem is still with us; prime rates are increasing. It won't be long before we're back to square one.
WELLS: Which makes it all the more important that Australian industry becomes competitive while we've got the time.
HARRIS: Ah, competition...
WELLS: That's right, Sir Leslie, the government can no longer afford to pump millions more dollars, propping up—
HARRIS: Spare me the rhetoric, Mr Wells. We employ seven thousand people in this state and another twenty thousand are directly dependent on us for their livelihood. Let me be blunt: if we can't make a profit, those people are going to find themselves without jobs.
WELLS: If you can't make a profit after forty years of government protection, subsidy and assistance—
HARRIS: Oh, dear me, fancy that. The socialists are trying to make honest capitalists out of us. Didn't you hear me, Mr Wells? I said twenty-seven thousand people!
WELLS: And I said, if you weren't competent enough to make a profit, don't expect the government to bail you out!
HARRIS: I never expected to be told how to do business by a government that can't even run a railway without losing a million dollars a day.
WELLS: There might be a few more surprises in store for you, Sir Leslie.
HARRIS: We donated one hundred thousand dollars to the union campaign to keep you in power—
WELLS: You donated that money to keep your own industrial relations under control!
HARRIS: And we expect something for our money.
WELLS: You haven't got much in return for your investments in the Liberal Party.
HARRIS: You've had your spies out, Michael. I suppose that's no surprise —you people seem to thrive on double dealing and intrigue.

WELLS: We've had good teachers, Sir Leslie.
HARRIS: [*to* CAREW] I can remember him as a young organiser. He was always so deferential. [*To* WELLS] The question is very simple: does the government want a heavy metal industry or not?
WELLS: Not one that's only an excuse for lining the pockets of titled bludgers.

A slight pause.

HARRIS: What do you want?
WELLS: We want an honest—
HARRIS: Honest? Did I really hear this government talking about honesty? We'll sack two hundred men every week until those mills and factories are a stinking corpse under your nose, and then we'll see what's left of your image as responsible economic managers.
WELLS: You do that, and every worker in this state will be calling for your nationalisation.
HARRIS: If you can come up with three and a half billion dollars, Mr Wells, you're quite welcome to it.
WELLS: You're kidding! The state has paid for every nut and bolt in that place three times over!
HARRIS: If you want to nationalise, that's what you'll pay.
WELLS: Maybe your shareholders are so fed up with your management they'll accept the next takeover offer.
HARRIS: No-one in Australia is big enough to take us over, Michael.
WELLS: You've been throwing your weight around for a long time, Sir Leslie, but this time you're wasting your breath.
HARRIS: I was here before you, Wells, and I'll be here after you. Funny about that Graham White chap, wasn't it?
WELLS: Who?
HARRIS: That North Coast developer who was supposed to have committed suicide—I'm sure you remember him. He gave you a cheque for seven thousand dollars at a fundraising party, but somehow it got lost. I don't think you've forgotten that.
WELLS: What about him?
HARRIS: It seems there's more to his death than meets the eye.
WELLS: Is that so?
HARRIS: Yes. In fact I found it so intriguing I hired a private investigation

ACT TWO

firm to follow it up. Its first report is very interesting—I'll send you a copy.

A slight pause.

WELLS: Are you trying to blackmail this government?

HARRIS: No, it couldn't come at a worse time, could it? A pity you can't keep yourselves as honest as you'd like other people to be. [*Preparing to exit*] I can't say it's been pleasant— I'd appreciate a phone call when you've made up your mind. Tell me, Mr Carew, what do you think of the way we do business in Australia?

A slight pause.

CAREW: Interesting.

HARRIS: I thought you'd feel right at home, I've had to deal with the teamsters on the odd occasion.

CAREW: They're a rough crowd.

HARRIS: Everyone can be rough, Mr Carew. [*To* WELLS] I'll be expecting that call.

HARRIS *exits. Pause.*

WELLS: Did you know he had private investigators snooping around?

CAREW: They don't know anything.

WELLS: They know about the seven thousand dollars!

CAREW: So does every journalist who hangs around the King's Arms.

WELLS: Do you know what they've got?

CAREW: Nothing. Gossip. You people certainly generate a lot of rumours, Michael.

WELLS: Have you seen the report?

CAREW: Relax, I know these jackasses. They don't know anything any paper in the country'd publish.

WELLS: Harris thinks he's got something.

CAREW: He was bluffing. The worst mistake you made was to look scared.

WELLS: Scared! Don't you know what this could mean if it came out?

CAREW: You shouldn't have mentioned anything about takeovers.

WELLS: We don't need this now!

CAREW: I'm handling it.

WELLS: Sometimes I wonder what kind of game you're playing.

CAREW: What do you mean by that?
WELLS: Why didn't you warn me? Did you know he was going to bring it up?
CAREW: Instead of worrying about that you'd be better trying to do something about Fitzgerald.
WELLS: I am.
CAREW: What? You told me he'd never make a deal with Palmer. If that's—
WELLS: It doesn't matter because we're going to win the union election, isn't that right?
CAREW: I think we might have to revise our positions after what Harris has just said.
WELLS: You told me it was sewn up!
CAREW: If they're going to start sacking two hundred men a week, Michael, I'd say there was a wild card in the pack.
WELLS: Jesus Christ.
CAREW: Give him the temporary assistance.
WELLS: How? BHP's already accepted the plan!
CAREW: Cook up some special considerations.
WELLS: I want that company bankrupt!
CAREW: Personal vendettas don't make good politics.
WELLS: Does TransOcean want it or not?
CAREW: I don't know who you think I am, but I'm not a representative of TransOcean.

A slight pause.

WELLS: If you think you can extract concessions out of me so that one bloodsucker replaces another on the economy of this country—
CAREW: You're not listening to me.
WELLS: Who are you a representative of?
CAREW: I said temporary assistance!
WELLS: That's what they've been saying for the last forty years!
CAREW: I don't think you're being very realistic, Michael.
WELLS: I think you're greatly understating your interests in this.
CAREW: What are they?
WELLS: You need me. You need my influence. If I go, who will you be dealing with?
CAREW: I'll deal with whoever I have to.

ACT TWO 37

WELLS: Fitzgerald? What do you think his attitude to the bases is? To Central America? To foreign investment?
CAREW: He seems sensible enough to see when compromise is needed.
WELLS: I won't compromise on this. I want to finish Harris off once and for all.
CAREW: Then I can't guarantee the election.
WELLS: You do your fucking job, mate. You fix the election and you fix Fitzgerald.

A slight pause.

CAREW: I might be able to do something.
WELLS: I hope so.
CAREW: It might not be what you'd like, but it'll keep the centre in power.
WELLS: That's all anybody wants.

The lights change.

SCENE TWO

The institute. Day.

The phone is ringing, someone is typing. JANE *and* ALLEN *enter on their way to a collective meeting.* ALLEN *carries a sheaf of handwritten notes.* ROSE *enters from the opposite side, carrying a shoulder bag.* ALLEN *does not immediately see her.*

ALLEN: Will somebody put on the answering machine?
JANE: She's a member of the Communist Party!
ALLEN: She's a collective member and therefore has the right to know.
JANE: They'll use the information against us at the board meeting.
ALLEN: Where will you use it against us?
JANE: I want this place to remain a viable alternative, Allen.
ALLEN: Then why are you trying to introduce sectarian politics into it?
JANE: You can't get any more fucking sectarian than the Communist Party!
ALLEN: There can't be any secrets between collective members! If we're going to run a deficit, they've got the right to know why.
JANE: It's not a matter of principle. Don't you know they're trying to take the board over?
ALLEN: Putting a spoke in your wheels, are they?

JANE: You'd let that happen just to get rid of me, wouldn't you?

ALLEN: This is a democratically organised workplace. No-one has the right to withhold information from anyone else.

JANE: I'll see you in the meeting. Maybe there's some other information they'd be interested in.

    JANE *exits.*

ALLEN: [*calling after her*] Like what, Jane? Like you've been using our account to have your party leaflets printed up?

    A slight pause.

ROSE: I thought collectives were supposed to be happy visions of the future.

ALLEN: Do I look unhappy? This is one of the fun places to work. What can I do for you, or have you already got your story?

ROSE: Unfortunately the machinations of the Institute of Applied Economics isn't a top priority at *Business Review*.

ALLEN: Why not? Me and the comrades are totally transforming the Australian business environment. It's about time we got a bit of media coverage.

ROSE: How about 'Left Splits Again'?

ALLEN: Hey, what is it with you? Are you a kind of latter-day Lauren Bacall?

ROSE: Why do you say that?

ALLEN: You seem to ooze this air of mysterious sensuality like a fucking squid's ink or some damn thing.

ROSE: Do you usually make instant judgements of people?

ALLEN: That's the sort of thing—answering a question with a question. I bet you'd be a good poker player.

ROSE: Are you angry with me?

    A slight pause.

ALLEN: No.

ROSE: Then don't get smart, I might bite your head off.

ALLEN: I already know one praying mantis at least— Look, I've got a fight I've got to sort out…

ROSE: Got time for a coffee later on?

ALLEN: How about a drink after work?

ROSE: What time?

ALLEN: Six, six-thirty.
ROSE: I'll meet you back here.

> *A very slight pause.*

ALLEN: [*pointing*] That's my office over there.
ROSE: Good.

> *She exits. A slight pause. The lights change. There is the dull noise of the mill in the background.*

SCENE THREE

Some waste ground at the steel mill. Day.

RAMON, DOUG, BRUCE *and* OTHERS *stand in a loose, half-hearted group. There is a feeling of despondency that hardens into antagonism.*

RAMON: You let your comrades get the sack and you don't do nothing. What sort of men are you?
FIRST WORKER: They stopped sackin' 'em! The government stopped 'em!
RAMON: They stop in BHP because they already got rid of everyone they want.
SECOND WORKER: They said no more retrenchments!
RAMON: Not here they didn't.
FIRST WORKER: We'll get the same deal.
RAMON: You want the same deal, do you? You've already had accidents because you're understaffed. They'll cut this workforce in half; they make the ones who are left produce twice as much.
FIRST WORKER: There's nothing we can do.

> *A gust of wind blows.*

RAMON: I never saw men like you, beaten before you even fight.
DOUG: What do you know? You don't even work here!

> *Two* WORKERS *are talking together, ignoring the others.*

RAMON: Why are you angry with me? If you're angry, why isn't it with Sir Leslie Harris?
DOUG: We've heard it all before, that's why. Every time there's a union election some bozo's around the place tellin' us what we should and shouldn't do. I been here thirty years; I learnt more from dunny walls than I ever did from you blokes.

RAMON: What are you going to do, then?
DOUG: I'm gonna do my job!
RAMON: How will you do that when everyone else is losing theirs?
DOUG: You don't care about them. All you want is to get elected.
RAMON: I care, mate.
FIRST WORKER: It's not the company's fault there's a recession.
RAMON: Is it yours? You're the one paying for it?
DOUG: [*moving off*] I've heard enough. Let's go.

> DOUG *and* BRUCE *leave. All except one follow.*

RAMON: You learnt nothing all your life! They said there'd never be another depression. This is no recession. This is a depression! They said they could control the capitalist economy. They said there are no classes in this country. They said this is a democracy where prosperity will be shared by all! Where are these things? Where are these beautiful lies?

> *There is another gust of wind.*

What's wrong with you? Have you let them kill your souls?
FIRST WORKER: We're men.
RAMON: Are men like this?

> *The lights change; all sound effects stop.*

SCENE FOUR

The institute. Late afternoon.

ALLEN *and* ROSE *enter. A slight pause.*

ALLEN: Could you turn on the light?
ROSE: Where is…?

> *A slight pause; the lights come up.*

How could you work in this darkness?
ALLEN: It's traditional. Is it still raining?
ROSE: Why don't you clean your windows? You might be able to see something.
ALLEN: If you knew what was out there you'd understand why.
ROSE: I know what's out there.
ALLEN: There's a pub nearby. Do you want to go there?

ACT TWO

ROSE: Do you have anything here?
ALLEN: Whisky? No ice.
ROSE: That's the way I like it. [*Seeing the crucifix*] A cross—that's a funny thing for a communist to have on his wall.
ALLEN: Not if you know anything about communist history.

A slight pause.

ROSE: I like a realist.

ALLEN *goes to pour the drinks. Pause.*

ALLEN: So where do you come from?
ROSE: You get personal very quickly.
ALLEN: Sorry, I must have got caught up in the ambience of the 'full and frank' discussions that are sweeping the country.

A slight pause.

ROSE: Where do I come from?
ALLEN: I'm not sure.
ROSE: Have a guess.
ALLEN: Middle class. Private school.
ROSE: Oh, history! I don't know why people bother with that.
ALLEN: What did you think I was talking about?
ROSE: How old are you?

A slight pause.

ALLEN: I'll be forty this year.
ROSE: Are the most important things that ever happened in your life the class you were born into and the school you attended?
ALLEN: [*giving her a glass*] What are the important things that have happened in your life?
ROSE: [*walking up to a reproduction*] I like Bosch too. Is this your favourite?
ALLEN: I'm not a communist.
ROSE: Aren't you? What are you, then?
ALLEN: A Marxist.
ROSE: A Marxist is only a communist who wants to pretend Stalin never existed.
ALLEN: Stalin existed.
ROSE: Then how can you be a Marxist?

ALLEN: Because I was dropped on my head by the priest when I was baptised. What sort of question's that?

A slight pause.

ROSE: Did you win your fight today?
ALLEN: Yes.
ROSE: Did it make you feel good?
ALLEN: Is this an in-depth interview?
ROSE: Not yet.
ALLEN: I don't have the time—
ROSE: Why not? What else have you got to do?
ALLEN: What do you want?
ROSE: I want to know why you're a Marxist.
ALLEN: Why?
ROSE: Maybe I want to be converted.
ALLEN: Go to church.
ROSE: You studied for the priesthood, didn't you?
ALLEN: What are you so nervous about?
ROSE: I find you intriguing: a cross on one wall and 'The Temptation of St Anthony' on the other.
ALLEN: I'm a psycho.
ROSE: You're an atheist.
ALLEN: Maybe atheists take morality more seriously than anyone else.
ROSE: I don't, and I'm an atheist. You're not suggesting there's a moral order out there?
ALLEN: The decisions you make are purely functional?
ROSE: How can you deal with people like Michael Wells and Charlie Palmer from a—?
ALLEN: What do you want?
ROSE: I want to know why you're a Marxist.
ALLEN: I'm a Marxist because I've got enough intellectual integrity to recognise the most elementary facts about how this society works. What are you? Instead of slipping and sliding around, how about putting your own assumptions on display so we can have a look at them?
ROSE: You've read my articles.
ALLEN: I was giving you the benefit of the doubt.

ACT TWO 43

ROSE: I thought you liked them; or was that just a party line?
ALLEN: Have you ever heard of Piero Sraffa?
ROSE: No.
ALLEN: Read him. The assumptions you make in your articles about how the economic world works have been demonstrably false for twenty years. Why are you a journalist? What are you doing with your life?
ROSE: I don't think you understand what I mean.
ALLEN: What do you mean?
ROSE: Marxism isn't just a system of analysis.
ALLEN: Neither's monetarism.
ROSE: Are you so confident you've got the truth, you'd kill people?
ALLEN: Do you know how many people were killed in Chile to impose the monetarist experiment? Do you know how many people in England—?
ROSE: That's not—
ALLEN: Don't accuse me of being a butcher when the whole history of the bourgeoisie from the enclosure movement to El Salvador has been one of slaughter! The socialists didn't commit the genocide in this country against the Aboriginal people!
ROSE: The capitalists didn't murder six million kulaks in Russia, either, Allen. Everyone can play that game.
ALLEN: You seem to have conceded you don't have the moral or intellectual right to print the stuff you do. Why do you do it?
ROSE: We're on two different wavelengths.
ALLEN: I know; you've already indicated that you've transcended the need to think and—
ROSE: Seeing that we're name-dropping, have you ever heard of Silvio Marti?
ALLEN: No.
ROSE: I didn't think you would; not many people have. He was a fourteen-year-old Christian Democrat. I saw his guts being ripped out while he was dragged down some dirty little back street in Salvador behind a car driven by leftist guerrillas. Just to put you in the picture a bit more, I was shot up by Christians a month later because they mistook me for the wife of a socialist shopkeeper. I'd show you the scars, but I wouldn't want to confuse your ideology.
ALLEN: What were you doing? Sightseeing?

ROSE: I was trying to make sense of the world.
ALLEN: So you stuck your nose into something you don't understand and nearly got it shot off. What's the lesson? Latin America isn't all hot tamale and jumping beans?
ROSE: That everything you've said is bullshit because it finally comes down to what human beings are like, and they're savages!
ALLEN: No! That's what you took with you from Sydney or New York or whatever other cosy hole you were occupying at the time.
ROSE: Don't knock it, there aren't too many cosy holes left.
ALLEN: I know, that's why I don't wash the windows.
ROSE: That's the way most people like their reality; but then again, most of them don't honour it by calling it a theory. I did have a reason for coming to see you.

She moves toward him, taking a piece of paper from her handbag.

ALLEN: You mean it wasn't just to swap jokes?
ROSE: When I got into work this morning, I found this in an envelope on my desk.

He takes it from her.

Have you ever heard of the company?
ALLEN: No— Why should I?
ROSE: I thought you might have come across it.
ALLEN: A balance sheet?
ROSE: Do you think Wells has any business interests?

A slight pause.

ALLEN: You did that interview with him last week.
ROSE: Do you?
ALLEN: You asked him that and he said no.
ROSE: What do you think?

A slight pause.

ALLEN: I've never been able to find... There's a Brisbane suburb called Milton— Have you tried the Queensland Register?
ROSE: Not yet.
ALLEN: Milton Imports. I've never heard of it.
ROSE: What do you think of the rumours of his drug involvement?
ALLEN: They're bullshit, he's not—

ACT TWO

ROSE: No-one is.
ALLEN: Even if he is a director, you don't know anything about the company.
ROSE: I know someone in the Narcotics Bureau.
ALLEN: If the Narcotics Bureau knew anything, someone would've told him to pull his head in.
ROSE: Or told the Bureau to pull their head in.

A slight pause.

ALLEN: When could you find out about this?
ROSE: Tomorrow. Would you like me to tell you what I come up with?

A slight pause.

ALLEN: Yes, I would.
ROSE: Isn't that dirty politics?
ALLEN: You didn't come here to talk about politics.
ROSE: What did I come here for?
ALLEN: I'm not sure. You don't believe in very much, do you?
ROSE: I don't believe in anything. [*Moving toward him*] Why did you invite me here?
ALLEN: We were going to have a drink.
ROSE: You're very good at evasion.
ALLEN: That's a compliment, coming from you.
ROSE: I'd like to know how far you're prepared to come with me.
ALLEN: How far are you going?
ROSE: To the end. I told you before, I'll destroy your soul.
ALLEN: Why would you want to do that?
ROSE: I need to find out which one of us is real.
ALLEN: It finally depends on what you want.
ROSE: Nobody knows what they want.
ALLEN: You must know what you want of me.
ROSE: Maybe I just want to use you.
ALLEN: I'm stronger than you are.
ROSE: I don't think so.
ALLEN: Try me.
ROSE: I'm going to fuck you.

The lights change.

SCENE FIVE

Allen's house. Night.
ALLEN *has his back turned to* LOUISE, *who is standing away from him.*

LOUISE: Allen?

    The lights change.

SCENE SIX

The backyard of Doug's house. Night.
ALLEN, BRUCE *and* DOUG *are sitting on their haunches, or stools,* DOUG *a little away from the other two. He has a plate of salad which he is eating with his fingers.* EILEEN *and* LOUISE *enter with plates.*

EILEEN: [*to* LOUISE] It's kosher.
LOUISE: I'm not.
ALLEN: [*to* BRUCE] I don't know why it rains, it just makes it more humid.
BRUCE: Yeah.
EILEEN: [*over* BRUCE] Yes, isn't it muggy? [*To* DOUG] Don't eat with your fingers, love. I brought out a knife and fork for you.
BRUCE: Where's the tomato sauce?
EILEEN: [*turning towards the house*] Oh, I left it inside.
BRUCE: [*forestalling her*] I'll get it.
LOUISE: [*to* EILEEN] Let him get it, he's a big boy.

    BRUCE *exits.*

EILEEN: [*settling*] He's been at work all day. The old bones have started to creak.
ALLEN: Have you got somewhere to sit, Mum?
EILEEN: I'll just sit over here with my daughter-in-law.
LOUISE: Us women have got to stick together.
EILEEN: That's right. Wasn't it hot today! What did it get to at the hearth, Doug?
DOUG: Hundred 'n' two in the lunch room.
LOUISE: How can you work in heat like that?
DOUG: You do.
LOUISE: But aren't there health regulations?

EILEEN: Did you see how much the grapevine has grown, Louise? We'll get grapes off it next year.
LOUISE: It's getting very big.
EILEEN: You should've pruned it when I told you, Doug. We might have had grapes this year.
DOUG: You don't prune a vine as young as that.
EILEEN: You do! Mrs Campadelli said you've got to prune it from the very first year.
BRUCE: [*re-entering*] Oh, what would she know? She just got out of the nuthouse!
EILEEN: She's got beautiful vines! And you shouldn't say things like that.
BRUCE: It's true, isn't it?
EILEEN: You don't know what sort of worries she's got.

A slight pause.

LOUISE: Is that the vine you got in Bathurst?
EILEEN: Yes, from Doug's father's house—Joe Fitzgerald.
LOUISE: That's where you were born, Mr Fitzgerald.

A slight pause.

DOUG: Yeah.
ALLEN: There wouldn't be much there now, would there, Dad?
DOUG: Just the chimney and the fruit trees.
EILEEN: But you can't eat anything off them, they're all flyblown and stony.
BRUCE: [*to* ALLEN] Hey, Allen, I thought you said you wanted to go up one weekend 'n' have a look at it.
ALLEN: I do.
BRUCE: How about Queen's Birthday?
ALLEN: Maybe.
BRUCE: What do you mean, maybe? Do ya want to or not?
ALLEN: I'm not sure I can—I'll have to look up my diary.
BRUCE: Diary? Geez.
EILEEN: You haven't been there yet, have you, Louise?
LOUISE: Not yet.
EILEEN: We found a grave up there last Christmas. [*To* DOUG] I'm sure it must be great-great-grandfather's, Doug. [*To* LOUISE] It said he was born in County Clare, Ireland; and died in 1848.

LOUISE: [*to* ALLEN] Now there's a year!
BRUCE: Hey, Dad, he must've come out in the gold rushes, don't you reckon?
DOUG: No, before that.
EILEEN: That tourist brochure said gold wasn't discovered there till 1851.
BRUCE: Maybe he got lost.
EILEEN: I reckon he was a fighting Irishman who got transported for the wearing of the green. That's us, the Fighting Fitzgeralds. [*Referring to* ALLEN] That's where he gets his bad blood from.
BRUCE: He probably just got drunk and caught the wrong train.
LOUISE: I thought Fitzgerald was an English name.
EILEEN: It was a big headstone, like he was someone important.
DOUG: Dad used to say we used to own a lot of land out there.
LOUISE: Did he say what happened to the Aboriginals who owned it before?
BRUCE: There weren't any out there, were there, Dad?

A slight pause.

DOUG: I s'pose they killed them.
BRUCE: Yeah, but only because they were killin' sheep, or somethin'.
LOUISE: What kind of excuse is that? They were defending their land.
BRUCE: They hadn't done nothin' with it!
LOUISE: Great! So you would've welcomed the Japanese invasion because they might do something with the country. Sure.
EILEEN: Calm down, the two of you— Oh, look; there's a shooting star.

A slight pause.

BRUCE: We're doin' somethin'.
LOUISE: Yeah, turning it into a desert.
EILEEN: Did you see that documentary on television the other night?
LOUISE: No, what about?
EILEEN: It was about the desert coming in over the farmland. Wasn't it frightening, Doug?
BRUCE: [*to* LOUISE] How are we turning it into desert?
LOUISE: It's all that intensive farming and overstocking. They're destroying the soil. The same thing happened in the US in the thirties: that's what *The Grapes of Wrath* is about.
EILEEN: Wasn't it a pity about Henry Fonda dying?

LOUISE: There's no cover on the soil now. All it needs is a big wind and it'll blow it all away, and that'll be the end. It'll be just like the badlands in America.
EILEEN: You're brainy, Allen, what's going on?
ALLEN: It's the end of the world.
BRUCE: But—how can you blame the drought on the farmers?
LOUISE: I'm not blaming the drought on the farmers. All I'm saying is that the methods they use to maximise their profits are destroying the land's ability to withstand drought.
EILEEN: Man's greed.

A slight pause.

DOUG: There's people out there still living on dirt floors.
EILEEN: But they overstock, Doug, you've said that yourself.
DOUG: It's not because they're greedy.
LOUISE: No, it's because they're semi-serfs mortgaged to the bank and the meat companies and they're too stupid to see how they're getting screwed.
ALLEN: We're trying to eat, Louise!
EILEEN: Will you be able to get up for Easter, Louise?
LOUISE: No—
ALLEN: No, we're going away, Mum.
EILEEN: Oh, where are you going?
ALLEN: We're going camping up the coast.
EILEEN: That'll be nice— But you should come and celebrate Easter with us. If it is the end of the world, it might be your last chance to be saved.
LOUISE: Allen's saved himself.
ALLEN: Was that gold prospector you knew still up there, Dad?

A slight pause.

DOUG: No. He died.
EILEEN: We met a young couple with a little two-year-old panning for gold on the Campbell River. They were lovely, weren't they, Doug?

A very slight pause.

DOUG: He was out of work—motor mechanic. They were just using a dish. There's no gold left there.
EILEEN: He got a few specks when you showed him how.

DOUG: It was cleaned out a hundred years ago. You need proper mining equipment now. There was hardly enough water in the river to even wash a dish of gold.
EILEEN: The country's terribly dry, Louise, it'd break your heart. The poor starving animals. There was a baby lamb that must have got separated from its mother. We stopped and tried to pick some grass for it off the side of the road, but it must have been too young to eat it. It just kept crying for its mother.
DOUG: She must've been dead. I couldn't find her anywhere.
LOUISE: What did you do?

A slight pause.

DOUG: I broke its neck.
EILEEN: [*excitedly to* ALLEN] Oh! I didn't tell you, Allen! I don't know what I must've been thinking about. That first Fitzgerald, the one whose grave we found, you'll never guess what his name was.
ALLEN: Stokely Carmichael.
EILEEN: No, stupid— Who's he? Allen. Allen Patrick Fitzgerald.
ALLEN: It must have been me.
BRUCE: Haven't you been feelin' too healthy lately, mate?
ALLEN: No—and I thought it was just because the phone bill had come in.

The lights change.

SCENE SEVEN

Doug's backyard. Night.

ALLEN, DOUG *and* BRUCE *are talking.* DOUG *is rolling a cigarette. A slight pause. He looks at the sky.*

DOUG: It's a full moon.

A slight pause.

ALLEN: Dad said you had an accident at work.

A slight pause.

BRUCE: Yeah… We're two men down.
DOUG: You shouldn't have been on that side, Bruce.
BRUCE: Someone had to be over there.

DOUG: Never think you know everything.

A slight pause.

BRUCE: [*to* ALLEN] The foreman told Dad maybe he should retire early.

A slight pause.

ALLEN: Or get the sack?
DOUG: They'd have to close the whole place before they got me.
BRUCE: They put off Jim Mackie last week.
DOUG: He was in the stores—that's another section.
ALLEN: [*to* BRUCE] What's he going to do?
BRUCE: What can he do? He's the same age as Dad.
ALLEN: [*to* DOUG] How's he taking it?
DOUG: He's alright. He was at the St Vincent De Paul Society meeting on Thursday.
BRUCE: We might be delivering a Christmas hamper to his place this year.
DOUG: They'll come over and eat with us the way they always do.
BRUCE: Will you give him another job, Dad?
DOUG: Allen doesn't want to hear our worries. Come and have a look at the carnations your mother planted.

He bends down.

Look at that—the tulips are coming up again. I thought I dug them all up… It's Frank's anniversary next week.

ALLEN: I know.

DOUG mimes picking a carnation, coughs bronchially and stands.

DOUG: Carnations are your mother's favourite flower, I don't know why she never planted them before…

He puts it in ALLEN*'s lapel.*

There; just like when you were married.

He puts his arm around ALLEN *and turns them both to face* BRUCE *as if for a wedding photograph.*

He's just the same, isn't he, Bruce?

DOUG pats ALLEN *and lets him go.*

Will you be coming down for the mass?
ALLEN: Yes.

DOUG: The chaplain from his platoon is going to say it. Did Bruce tell you about his girlfriend?

ALLEN: No.

DOUG: He hasn't brought her home yet. Maybe next week— I think your mother'd like to meet her. [*To* ALLEN] So how are things, son? [*To* BRUCE] Bruce, get me a cordial. [*Back to* ALLEN] Do you want a cordial? Something to drink?

ALLEN: No thanks, Dad.

DOUG: [*to* BRUCE] See if there's some ice.

> BRUCE *exits. A slight pause.*

How are you?

ALLEN: I'm fine, Dad.

DOUG: You're tense, what are you worried about?

ALLEN: Nothing.

DOUG: How's your work?

ALLEN: Good.

DOUG: Is everything alright between you and Louise?

ALLEN: Everything's alright.

> *A slight pause.*

DOUG: I don't think so. Every time she looked at you tonight, you looked away. What is it?

> *A slight pause.*

ALLEN: She had no right to attack Bruce the way she did.

DOUG: No she didn't, but…

> *A slight pause.*

He can look after himself… I've been worried about you two for a while. You've only been married six years but to look at you you'd think it was a hundred and six. You don't act the way young married people should.

ALLEN: How should they act, Dad?

DOUG: Don't get sarcastic with me, son: you might be thirty-nine, but I'm still your father.

> *A slight pause.*

ALLEN: I didn't mean—

ACT TWO

DOUG: Just tell me what's on your mind.
ALLEN: It's different…
DOUG: What's different?
ALLEN: Men and women are different.
DOUG: Don't they fall in love anymore? Don't they like to hold hands?

A slight pause.

ALLEN: I can't explain…
DOUG: Are you seeing another woman?
ALLEN: No.

A slight pause.

DOUG: Do you still love Louise?
ALLEN: Yes, I do.
DOUG: Why don't you show it?
ALLEN: She doesn't want me to.
DOUG: Don't be stupid, man, every woman wants to know she's loved.
ALLEN: She wants to be independent, Dad. She doesn't want me to hold her hand in public; she doesn't want the two of us to go together on social occasions—
DOUG: She wants to be single.

A slight pause.

ALLEN: She wants her own life.

A slight pause.

DOUG: You're married, and you're the head of your family. She knew the obligations and responsibilities marriage would bring. If it's not working out, it's your fault for not being firm enough.
ALLEN: What can I do, Dad? Chain her to me?
DOUG: A woman needs a strong hand to rely on; if she doesn't have one, she's all over the place. It sounds to me that's what's happening to you two.

A slight pause.

ALLEN: She's an adult, Dad: she knows what she wants.
DOUG: Not if she wants to be married and single at the same time. How is she going to cope with motherhood?

ALLEN moves away.

Don't walk away from me when I'm talking to you. What kind of family do you want your children to be brought up in? Or doesn't she want to be tied down with children?

> BRUCE *returns, but seeing them talking, stops on the edge of the light. Pause.*

I asked you a question, son.
ALLEN: This is my problem, Dad; I'll handle it.
DOUG: You're not handling it, Allen, you're letting it get worse. You're my eldest son, and you're failing.
ALLEN: [*upset*] What can I do?
DOUG: You can be a man. She's just testing you to see if you love her. You lay down the law and she'll be a lot happier.
ALLEN: I'm not her master, Dad.
DOUG: If you want your family to survive, you'll have to learn to take responsibility for it.
ALLEN: Don't you think I'm trying?
DOUG: Trying's not good enough, you've got to succeed. If you want anything to happen in this world, you've got to make it. [*Seeing* BRUCE] What are you standing over there for? I'm dying of thirst.

> BRUCE *comes forward.*

Did you tell Allen you'd enrolled in the tech course?
BRUCE: He's not interested in that, Dad.
DOUG: A brother's always interested in what his brother's doing.
ALLEN: What are you doing?
BRUCE: [*quietly*] Electronics.
DOUG: If you'd wanted to be an electrician, you shoulda done an apprenticeship.
BRUCE: It's not the same as an electrician, Dad. It's buildin' radios 'n' computers 'n' things.
DOUG: Computers. [*To* ALLEN] Do you think he'll be able to build a computer?
BRUCE: I can do it.
DOUG: Maybe you can. You can do anything if you don't let it break your heart first.
BRUCE: I won't let it break my heart.
DOUG: Good. Then you'll beat it, won't he, Allen?

ALLEN: Yes, Dad.

The lights change.

SCENE EIGHT

The kitchen of Doug's house. Night.

EILEEN *is drying her hands on a dish towel;* LOUISE *is holding some plates. As becomes apparent,* LOUISE *is quite tense.*

LOUISE: Do you think they'll keep their jobs?

EILEEN: I don't know, it's a worry. Don't bother putting them away, Louise, I'll do it later. Well, that's that finished for another night. There's trouble all over the world, isn't there? Those new diseases in America, wars, revolutions— It makes you wonder sometimes.

LOUISE: Revolution might be the only hope for some people.

EILEEN: Why do people have to kill one another?

LOUISE: Maybe they don't have any choice.

EILEEN: But you can change things without violence. Did you see *Gandhi*?

LOUISE: No.

EILEEN: He didn't use violence. He was one of the most peaceful men in the world.

LOUISE: If you can bring about change without violence, all the better, but sometimes there's no other way.

EILEEN: Could you kill someone?

LOUISE: I don't know. Could you?

A slight pause.

EILEEN: I don't think I could live with myself if I'd killed someone.

LOUISE: What if someone attacked your children?

A slight pause.

EILEEN: Yes, I could kill then.

LOUISE: Where did you say to put the plates, Mrs Fitzgerald?

EILEEN: Call me Eileen, Louise. And I think Dad would rather you call him Doug.

LOUISE: Alright—Eileen.

EILEEN: Just put them down on the table. Well, wasn't that nice? I'm glad you came up; it's good to have the family together.

LOUISE: You should come down to our place sometime. I've just painted the living room.
EILEEN: You know what Doug's like, he likes his own home. How much longer do you think you'll be working for before you settle down?
LOUISE: We're not going to settle down.
EILEEN: You'll have to sometime. Oh, you're joking. You almost had me fooled for a minute. But wouldn't it be nice to have your own home and garden?
LOUISE: Yes, I suppose.
EILEEN: A place that was your own instead of paying out rent all the time.

>   LOUISE *sings softly from Bruce Springsteen's 'I'm a Rocker'.*

There might be children. You need your security.
LOUISE: That's what my mother used say.
EILEEN: That's what all mothers say, and they're right.
LOUISE: She went mad.
EILEEN: Yes, poor soul. But she had a nice house.
LOUISE: We're doing what we like, Eileen—we're happy.
EILEEN: You wait till you get old. Allen's going to be forty this year, you'll be thirty. Your time's running out for having children. It's alright to kick up your heels when you're a teenager, but you don't stay young forever.
LOUISE: Well, they might drop the bomb next year and put an end to all our worries.
EILEEN: But just in case they don't, you should take out a mortgage now.
LOUISE: But think of the bargains if we wait!
EILEEN: Yes! You might get Parliament House for a song! I don't know, Louise. We had to bring up our kids with someone threatening to bomb someone else every time you turned on the radio. You just have to ignore it.
LOUISE: You should have been a Jew.
EILEEN: Wouldn't I look nice at Christmas.
LOUISE: We know what we're doing with our lives, Eileen.

>   *A very slight pause.*

EILEEN: Louise—did I…?

LOUISE: I'm sorry for fighting with Bruce. I didn't… I didn't mean it.
EILEEN: I just want you to be happy.
LOUISE: I know.

   A slight pause.

EILEEN: Allen used to say that, used to scream that at me, 'I know what I'm doing! I know what I'm doing!'—but he didn't. He studies to be a priest, and ends up an atheist; he fights to become a professor, and ends up earning less than his father; he wants peace and happiness in the world, and tries to commit suicide. Sometimes it's like watching a man struggling to the death with himself.
LOUISE: Men try, women succeed.

   A very slight pause.

EILEEN: Is something the matter, Louise?
LOUISE: Are you happy?
EILEEN: Have I done something? Said something?
LOUISE: No— In yourself; are you happy?
EILEEN: Yes. Why?
LOUISE: Every time we see each other we end up talking about exactly the same things.
EILEEN: [*uncertainly*] What would you rather talk about?
LOUISE: I'm sorry, I'm not attacking you.
EILEEN: What's wrong? I'm happy to have a daughter-in-law I can talk to… Louise?
LOUISE: My mother went mad in a nice house and a loving family because nothing… No-one ever paid the slightest attention to anything she wanted or had the slightest idea of who she was. I don't want that to happen to me, Eileen. Is that too much to ask?

   A slight pause.

EILEEN: Are you and Allen fighting?
LOUISE: We're fine, Eileen, really. Maybe we should go and join the others.
EILEEN: Why don't you like visiting us, Louise?

   A slight pause.

LOUISE: Because I'm not a part of this.

EILEEN: Don't we make you welcome? Don't we love you?
LOUISE: Yes. Thank you.
EILEEN: Then what is it?
LOUISE: Why is the woman in that picture exposing her heart?
EILEEN: [*faltering*] That's Our Lady, the Mother of Our Lord. That's the way Bernadette saw her, with her heart full of tears for the world.
LOUISE: Is that what women are like?
EILEEN: Women—are the ones who weep.
LOUISE: Let's go outside with the others.
EILEEN: It's not a fight, Louise.
LOUISE: I can't talk any more, Eileen—
EILEEN: I'm sorry, Louise... I'm sorry.

The lights change.

SCENE NINE

Allen's house. Night.

ALLEN *and* LOUISE *enter arguing.*

ALLEN: How dare you attempt to provoke a fight with my brother in my father's house.
LOUISE: In that Christian mausoleum! Why is that religion so obsessed with death?
ALLEN: Are you incapable of accepting people's generosity without spitting in their faces?
LOUISE: Why are you doing this to me? You don't believe a word you're saying.
ALLEN: They're my parents.
LOUISE: And I'm your wife!
ALLEN: You've accepted that now.
LOUISE: How can you sit there and listen to those things without seeing and hearing what they're about?
ALLEN: I'm sensitive to the feelings of my mother and father!
LOUISE: No, I haven't accepted it. Not your definition.
ALLEN: Yours doesn't correspond to anything in the real world.
LOUISE: You're numb! They could tell you God wanted your sacrifice and you'd put your head on the block.

ALLEN: That's their religion! Haven't they got a right to their beliefs?
LOUISE: It's not just their religion. It's everything they do. The way they think and feel.
ALLEN: What's wrong with that?
LOUISE: They're still living in the Middle Ages! It's fascism!
ALLEN: Is that what you think as you eat their food?
LOUISE: Why can't you see it? The crosses on the walls! The lords and ladies standing over them!
ALLEN: Is that what you said to my mother? Is that why she was upset?
LOUISE: You don't care about your mother. You're happy to have her serve you hand and foot.
ALLEN: I love her!
LOUISE: If you loved her you'd weep for what that culture has done to her.
ALLEN: I don't want to listen to this!
LOUISE: Why are you going to a mass for a brother who's been dead fifteen years when you don't believe in the soul?
ALLEN: Out of respect for them!
LOUISE: You respect them but you treat me as though I'm mad.
ALLEN: They're not flying in the face of every human intuition and emotion.
LOUISE: It's a barbaric celebration of the warrior son! A glorification of—
ALLEN: [*over her*] He's my brother!
LOUISE: —war and masculinity! He's dead!
ALLEN: What do we do? Just forget them? Leave them in the ground to rot?
LOUISE: Have you ever once told your father what you think of him for sending Frank to Vietnam?
ALLEN: What's this got to do with simple manners in someone else's home?
LOUISE: Because I can't plug up my emotions the way you have. Why did you lie to them about why we weren't coming up for Easter?
ALLEN: I didn't want them to see I was married to an hysteric.
LOUISE: Instead of confronting it, Allen, you've just put up a wall of lies.
ALLEN: You can't change them. You don't have any right to try.
LOUISE: [*in anguished disbelief*] Then what are we socialists for?
ALLEN: Not to terrorise people out of their customs.

LOUISE: What? The family? The church? Militarism? They're all going to be in place after the revolution?
ALLEN: What have we got to offer instead? Do you see our relationship as a happy alternative to offer the people?
LOUISE: I won't be emotionally blackmailed by you!
ALLEN: Has socialism brought every worthwhile value into the world?
LOUISE: What could you possibly find valuable in that voodoo bag of misogyny and sadomasochism?
ALLEN: That religion gave me my first experience of morality!
LOUISE: It gave you an experience of subservience to anyone who called themselves 'Father'! Why do you think I rejected Judaism?
ALLEN: You can't. You're a Jew. You were born one and you think like one.
LOUISE: I don't want to! I don't want that oppression. I fight it in myself!
ALLEN: How can you cut yourself in half? How can you deny your history and your culture?
LOUISE: The culture they drove into Beirut in armoured personnel carriers?
ALLEN: The culture of Spinoza and Freud!
LOUISE: All I want is to find a place for myself!
ALLEN: You've got one: beside me!
LOUISE: I feel so lonely!
ALLEN: Then stop this mad crusade and come back to me!
LOUISE: I'm not mad! Stop saying it!
ALLEN: I can't stand the thought of you with her!
LOUISE: Why do you want me to hate you?
ALLEN: I want you to forgive me!
LOUISE: What have you done?

The lights change.

SCENE TEN

The institute. Day.

ALLEN *and* JANE *are present.*

JANE: ... We're three weeks behind with our IAC submission, the textile report hasn't even been started, the rank-and-file metalworkers—

ALLEN: Shut up!

   Pause.

   What is it you want out of me?

   A slight pause.

JANE: You've received a clear instruction from the collective to finish the metal industry report and get on with your other work.

ALLEN: Since when has it been your responsibility to tell the rest of us what to do?

JANE: The collective is telling you!

ALLEN: You're not the collective!

JANE: And you can't unilaterally decide which decisions you're going to respect and which you're going to ignore!

ALLEN: I'll decide when my work is finished!

JANE: Then how about telling the next meeting the reason they're snowed under is that you're trying to get yourself elected to the state executive of the—?

ALLEN: There is one thing I'd like to get clear at the next meeting! How many of them know you're having an affair with my wife? Or have you whispered it to them all?

   A slight pause.

JANE: I'm not having an 'affair' with your wife.

ALLEN: What do you call it?

JANE: You can't decide for her what relationship—

ALLEN: Don't give me that feminist crap: you're using her to undermine me here.

JANE: What gives you the right—?

ALLEN: I'm her husband!

   A slight pause.

JANE: I always thought you were just a little dictator—

ALLEN: Listen, you cunt. I don't like you and I don't like your politics. You keep out of my way, or I'll kill you.

   Pause.

JANE: You're finished here.

ALLEN: I mean it, Jane. Get out of that door and don't come back.

Pause. JANE *hesitates. The phone rings.* ALLEN *answers the phone;* JANE *exits.*

[*Into the phone*] Hello!... Bob who!... Oh, Bob... No, it's nothing but excitement. I don't suppose you're ringing to tell me to get my money out of the bank fast. How are you?... A drink? Sure, when?... No, I've got to see someone tonight— What about Thursday?... What's up?

RAMON *enters.*

Okay, see you then.... Yeah, 'bye.

He hangs up.

RAMON: Have you heard the news?
ALLEN: What?
RAMON: Go down and buy a paper! That bastard Harris is going to put off two hundred men a week because he says there's not enough protection! What protection do the workers have?

A slight pause.

ALLEN: They'll bring down the government.
RAMON: You should see the workers, my friend, they're really angry!
ALLEN: Well, you better get ready to hose them down.
RAMON: What's wrong? Didn't you hear me? They want a big fight!
ALLEN: I heard you.
RAMON: This will tip the scales for sure. Wells is finished.
ALLEN: I know.
RAMON: I was handing out leaflets at Glenville; I didn't have enough to give away. If we could only get your father's factory, we'd be home.
ALLEN: We're home anyway.
RAMON: I came to pick up your article for *Militant Voice*.
ALLEN: It's the orange folder.
RAMON: This is amazing, my friend: the first time the left has got a chance for forty years! Think of what we can do when we have the executive! Everything must change! We must get rid of the bureaucrats! We must start our own party paper and radio station and get debate going amongst the people! We must tell them the truth about what is happening!
ALLEN: Do you think they'll want to know?

ACT TWO

RAMON: They'll want to know everything. You'll be surprised when you see the people's strength! They don't know what it is to live like free men and women; they'll shake heaven and hell when they get up to dance.

A slight pause.

ALLEN: There is no heaven and there is no hell. That's what you said, Ramon.

RAMON: You talk funny, my friend. What's wrong?

ALLEN: Nothing. Everything's perfect.

The lights change.

SCENE ELEVEN

Doug's house. Afternoon.

EILEEN *is listening from a distance to* DOUG *and* BRUCE *as they take off their work clothes.*

BRUCE: Allen wouldn't get involved, Dad, if he didn't think it was good.

DOUG: I don't want to talk about it.

BRUCE: But that bloke was right: they're sacking everyone and we're not doing anything about it.

DOUG: It's their right.

BRUCE: Don't we have the right to work?

DOUG: We're working.

BRUCE: But what about everyone else—? What about Jim Mackie?

DOUG: Jim wouldn't want us to go on strike for him, and I wouldn't want anyone to do it for me.

BRUCE: Well, I would if I was tryin' to pay off a house and look after two kids.

DOUG: You're not.

BRUCE: What's it matter if I'm not, there's blokes who are. Aren't we s'posed to help each other?

DOUG: If you want to help you could do more work with St Vincent de Paul.

BRUCE: Who wants charity? They just want their jobs back!

DOUG: I want 'em to get their jobs back too; but I'm not gonna turn into a thug to do it.

BRUCE: All he's sayin', Dad, is the union leadership's no good and we need a change.
DOUG: A change that'll put the communists in charge.
BRUCE: Allen's not a communist!
DOUG: You're my son, and while you're in my house, you'll obey me!
BRUCE: Maybe I should move out!
DOUG: Maybe you should!
EILEEN: Doug!

The lights change.

SCENE TWELVE

A room. Night.

CAREW *is on the phone.*

CAREW: [*into the phone*] There's been a change of plans: we're going to have to dump him... Listen to me, will you?... I'm here, okay?... I know what's going on and I know what I can do about it!... Wells has gone ballistic, there's nothing we can do. We'll have to get rid of both of them.

The lights change.

SCENE THIRTEEN

The institute. Night.

ALLEN *and* ROSE *are together.*

ROSE: Nothing will ever change in this country.
ALLEN: You like things the way they are, do you? The madness.
ROSE: The madness is inside you.
ALLEN: So it's all an illusion.
ROSE: Other people live.
ALLEN: How?
ROSE: Day by day.

SCENE FOURTEEN

Bob's apartment. Night.

ACT TWO

BOB *and* JANICE.

JANICE: When can we talk?
BOB: I'm busy, I told you!
JANICE: I can't stand this, Bob! I feel like I'm living in solitary confinement, living with you!
BOB: [*holding up a report*] Don't you understand what this is? One of the largest takeover offers in the country's history!
JANICE: What's it got to do with us?
BOB: I suppose it depends on what kind of country you want to live in, doesn't it?
JANICE: I don't care what happens to the country! I care about what happens in my own house!

SCENE FIFTEEN

The nightmare continues.

ALLEN: And nothing changes.
ROSE: You get older.
ALLEN: Is that your only ambition?
ROSE: It's not an ambition at all. It's a fact.
ALLEN: A fact that negates everything else.
ROSE: No. Death does that.
ALLEN: So death is the only reality.
ROSE: You don't understand me, do you?
ALLEN: I know there's something you want.
ROSE: No, it's what you want. I don't want anything.
ALLEN: Why not?
ROSE: Because I've had it all. Power, hunger, fear, desire.
ALLEN: You don't seem any the worse for wear for it.
ROSE: It affects people in different ways. How will it affect you?
ALLEN: Do you think that's what I'm after?
ROSE: Yes.
ALLEN: [*voice-over, shouting*] No!
DOUG: [*illuminated*] You're my eldest son.
ALLEN: All I want is to control my life.
ROSE: You can't even control your emotions.

ALLEN: What makes you say that?
ROSE: You're married and you're falling in love with me.
ALLEN: What do you want me to do?
ROSE: It's not too late to run away.
ALLEN: Is this the contemporary version of the dance of death?
ROSE: No rationalisations, you're too good at that.
ALLEN: You want to take away my only defence?
ROSE: Of course. It's not a very good defence, anyhow.
ALLEN: Against what?
ROSE: The despair you feel.
ALLEN: I'm not in despair.
ROSE: Aren't you? I would be if I were you.
ALLEN: Why?
ROSE: Because you'll never get what you want.
ALLEN: No-one ever does.
ROSE: That's remarkably mature of you.
ALLEN: It doesn't stop you from fighting for it.

SCENE SIXTEEN

Night.

WELLS *walks to the phone and picks it up.*

WELLS: [*into the phone*] Dianne, get me Allen Fitzgerald, will you?

SCENE SEVENTEEN

ROSE: You've got a tragic view of life.
ALLEN: What do you want?
ROSE: I want to find out which one of us is real.
ALLEN: What are the positions?
ROSE: Any positions you like.
ALLEN: All for the adrenalin.
ROSE: Not all of it.
ALLEN: I want you.
ROSE: Everything you do is about control.
ALLEN: I need to know.
ROSE: Look for once at the chaos.

ALLEN: Who are you?
ROSE: Feel me!

> *All sound effects stop.*
>
> *A spotlight comes up on* ALLEN *and* ROSE *violently fucking;* ALLEN *comes, screaming.*
>
> *Blackout.*

END OF ACT TWO

ACT THREE

Blackout. The crashing sound of a train. A MAN's VOICE *is heard yelling: 'Heaven!' The glass wind bell tinkles.*

SCENE ONE

Wells' office. Night.
A slight pause.

WELLS: Hello, Allen.

A slight pause.

ALLEN: I've never been here before. I'm glad I've seen what you're losing.

A slight pause.

WELLS: What do you want?
ALLEN: It's too late—
WELLS: What do you want? A safe seat? Federal? State? What?
ALLEN: I want you out of here.
WELLS: You'll never shift me. If you want to make a deal, get that straight.
ALLEN: I don't want to make a deal—
WELLS: You feel more comfortable with Charlie Palmer, do you?
ALLEN: If that's all you asked me here for, save your breath.

Pause.

WELLS: What would you do if you had power?
ALLEN: The first thing we're going to do is democratise the party and—
WELLS: Don't give me the shits, Fitzgerald. What is it you're after?
ALLEN: Care to show me the books so I can see what the real lurks and perks are?
WELLS: Come on, I'm listening. You leftists are always complaining. What are you going to do?
ALLEN: Read the Alternative Economic Strategy if you're interested.
WELLS: What you blokes can't get through your heads is that Australia's capitalist, and all the forces of heaven and hell aren't going to change that.

ACT THREE

ALLEN: Maybe ordinary Australians will.
WELLS: What do you know about ordinary Australians?
ALLEN: I don't drive a Mercedes, Wells.
WELLS: Most ordinary Australians'd like to string bastards like you up from the nearest telegraph pole.
ALLEN: It must be a bit of a shock for you that we're winning. Why is that, Mike? Why is our strategy working and yours isn't?
WELLS: All your strategy is doing is threatening the stability of the government.
ALLEN: Is that what your American friends are telling you?
WELLS: I'll tell you you'll never gain power! If you win, the government'll fall—
ALLEN: Not again. We won't back down next time.
WELLS: The American alliance is central to Australian politics.
ALLEN: They're strangling our economy and our national life.
WELLS: If it wasn't for American capital we wouldn't have an economy.
ALLEN: The depression seems to have solved that particular problem.
WELLS: It's bottomed out.
ALLEN: It's just holding— Just waiting for the next international crash.
WELLS: What can we do? Budget deficits? We've already got the largest deficit in our history.
ALLEN: Socialise industry.
WELLS: What does that mean?
ALLEN: Nationalise without—
WELLS: We couldn't nationalise a milk bar, mate, even if we wanted to. They'd destroy us.
ALLEN: Who? Put a name on them!
WELLS: The Australian people.
ALLEN: No, the Australian capitalists. The bastards that have been suckin' on the nation since Macarthur wheedled his first sheep run out of the government.

A slight pause.

WELLS: You've got it all worked out: capitalists and workers. I suppose you realise workers only represent twenty-nine per cent of the population—
ALLEN: And it's decreasing all the time—
WELLS: What are you going to do about the sixty-seven per cent who are part of the middle class?

ALLEN: At the rate you're wiping them out I don't think we'll need to do anything.
WELLS: What do you think they're going to do? Where's the support for socialism?
ALLEN: We're on the brink, Wells. Australian society is never going to be the same again.
WELLS: I know about power and I know what's possible. Our only hope to get this country moving is to get capitalism working—
ALLEN: It doesn't work! That's what this depression is about!
WELLS: You're in the wrong fucking party, mate.
ALLEN: I'm in the party that's still got the demand for democratic control of the means of production in its platform!
WELLS: Try implementing it! See how long you last.
ALLEN: How long are you going to last with the unemployed smashing down the doors of parliament?
WELLS: We'll last!
ALLEN: How? Have you got the army primed up?
WELLS: We've got the policies!
ALLEN: After ASIO finishes purging the party you won't have any trouble unleashing the military.
WELLS: I won't let this country sink into anarchy.
ALLEN: I don't like being called a KGB agent, Mike.
WELLS: What's the difference between what you want and what they want?
ALLEN: I don't know what they want, but I want a society that's got no place for people like you.
WELLS: There'll always be people like me, Fitzgerald.
ALLEN: Then I guess we're gunna have to build better sewers.

A slight pause.

WELLS: I asked you here to make a deal, and I'm still prepared to make it.
ALLEN: That's generous of you. Are your numbers men finally getting the message through?
WELLS: I've taken Harris on— I've taken on the state's arch capitalist— If we don't have a united party, he'll smash us.
ALLEN: Do you think you'll be able to pull me into line by throwing us into a fight of your choice to secure your own power?

ACT THREE

WELLS: Don't let yourself get outflanked, Allen: it'd be a shame for you to start looking like a reactionary at this stage of the game.

A slight pause.

ALLEN: What's the deal?

A slight pause.

WELLS: You support me as secretary for another term, I'll drop the investigation into your branches and any charges. I'll make a safe federal seat available to you, and I'll put a moratorium on faction fighting until my retirement.

A slight pause.

ALLEN: What else?
WELLS: What else do you want?
ALLEN: The lot. You're through, Wells. You've got nothing left to offer.
WELLS: You haven't won yet, comrade.
ALLEN: You've got some last bit of shit you think's going to save you, do you?
WELLS: More than one, mate. I've got a whole bucketful I'd be delighted to dump over you and Palmer.
ALLEN: You haven't got much credibility left as far as Palmer goes.
WELLS: I tried to have him expelled. You stopped it.
ALLEN: I postponed it.
WELLS: My, you've grown up, Allen.
ALLEN: Cut the shit! If you've got something to say, say it.

A slight pause.

WELLS: Charlie Palmer ordered Graham White's murder.
ALLEN: Bullshit.
WELLS: It's not bullshit! He and White were running the North Coast heroin trade together. White doublecrossed him and Palmer had him killed.
ALLEN: So the seven thousand you pocketed didn't have anything to do with it.
WELLS: I never touched that money! Palmer was the one who had it and Palmer was the one who had White murdered.
ALLEN: How do you know?
WELLS: I found out. Why do you think I tried to get him out of the party?

ALLEN: Have you gone to the police?
WELLS: It was a fucking cop that did it! You think you know about Palmer: you don't know half of it. That rats' nest at the Petersville Council has got its finger in every piece of crime and corruption in the state!
ALLEN: And you've been protecting him!
WELLS: You're the one doing it now! How's that going to look when you make your challenge?
ALLEN: How are you going to explain withholding evidence of a murder?
WELLS: I only just found out!
ALLEN: We've been saying that for the last three years.
WELLS: And you were right. So why are you in partnership with him now?
ALLEN: You're not going to do this to me.
WELLS: It doesn't look good, does it, comrade? You won't join me to bring down Harris and you've got some dirty deal going with one of the state's biggest criminals. Who's on the right now?
ALLEN: You stopped every investigation we tried to initiate.
WELLS: You never had any evidence, but as soon as I found out I moved against him.
ALLEN: Okay, I haven't seen any evidence either.
WELLS: You've got my word, Allen, and that'll be good enough for the executive: this whole conversation is being taped. You now know what I know. What are you going to do about it?
ALLEN: I'm going to find out what your connection is with Milton Imports.
WELLS: What?
ALLEN: I was always curious how you could rub shoulders with Palmer. I should have just realised you were as crooked as one another.
WELLS: What are you talking about?
ALLEN: That you're personally involved in drug pushing through a company called Milton Imports.
WELLS: That's bullshit! Who told you that?
ALLEN: I guess I was just confused by the fact that you're still a churchgoer. I suppose you were praying for the souls of the addicts.
WELLS: I've never had any criminal involvement!
ALLEN: I know you have and I'm going to find out what it is. You scum! If I have to scour the earth myself to establish your guilt, I'll do it.

ACT THREE

WELLS: It's not true!
ALLEN: If you have any loyalty left to the party, get out, before we throw you out!
WELLS: You'll never get the chance, Fitzgerald. I'll wipe you and your organisation out!
ALLEN: What with, Wells? You're finished.
The lights change.

SCENE TWO

The Rank and File Co-ordinating Centre: a busy centre used by a number of left groups. Afternoon.
RAMON, ROBIN, BRUCE *and* OTHERS *are present.*

ROBIN: If it's a lockout they'll have to picket.
BRUCE: Is this the Rank and File place?
ROBIN: [*to* BRUCE] Who are you after?
BRUCE: The steelworkers' bloke.
ROBIN: That's him over there.
BRUCE: Thanks.
RAMON: Have the leaflets been delivered yet, Robin?
ROBIN: I'm not your secretary, comrade. No.
She exits.
RAMON: [*to* BRUCE] Women! What can I do for you, my friend?
BRUCE: I'm from the Austeel plant. I want to find out what you blokes are on about.
RAMON: [*shaking his hand*] I'm pleased to meet you. Come on inside and we can talk. Have I met you before?
BRUCE: I was at the meeting you called last week.
RAMON: What's your name?
BRUCE: Bruce. Bruce Fitzgerald.
RAMON: I'm Ramon— I know your brother.
BRUCE: Yeah.
RAMON: Did he send you over?
BRUCE: No. I came myself.
The lights change.

SCENE THREE

The corridor of a newspaper building. Day.

We hear office noise, the sound of a telex machine. ROSE *is walking along carrying a manilla folder.* ALLEN *is behind her.*

ALLEN: Rose!
ROSE: [*turning*] What are you doing here?
ALLEN: It's nice to see you, too.
ROSE: What do you want?
ALLEN: You were going to get in touch about that company.
ROSE: I'm busy, Allen.
ALLEN: I need to know.

A slight pause; she looks quickly behind her.

ROSE: Come in here.

The lights change.

SCENE FOUR

A room in the newspaper building. Day.

The telex machine is muffled. ALLEN *and* ROSE *enter. A slight pause.*

ALLEN: Storage rooms: my favourite meeting places.
ROSE: I don't want you coming around to my workplace.
ALLEN: Why? Does it cramp your style?
ROSE: What do you want?
ALLEN: Have you heard anything back from Brisbane?
ROSE: What's the rush?
ALLEN: Have you?
ROSE: Yes. Just now, as a matter of fact. It looks like you were right.

She hands him a copy of the telex from her folder.

ALLEN: [*reading*] Jesus…
ROSE: What?
ALLEN: Graham White. The two of them directors: Wells and White.
ROSE: What do you know about him?
ALLEN: I don't. They must have been partners… There was some kind of falling-out with Palmer… What do you know about White?

ACT THREE

ROSE: Why do you ask?
ALLEN: I'm tired of playing charades, Rose: could you tell me?

A slight pause.

ROSE: He was found dead a month ago and the official report was suicide—
ALLEN: I know that. What else?
ROSE: What have you heard?
ALLEN: I was just told he was murdered.
ROSE: Who told you that?
ALLEN: That must be the reason...
ROSE: The reason for what?
ALLEN: This is it! This is what you've been looking for!
ROSE: It's only a piece of paper.
ALLEN: Graham White was involved in the heroin trade, and here's fucking Wells sitting on the same board of directors with the bastard.
ROSE: You're a real puritan, aren't you?
ALLEN: The guy's a criminal!
ROSE: How do you know he was involved in the heroin trade?
ALLEN: What are you getting cold feet about? Here's your story!
ROSE: Graham White died a real estate developer, ruined by the recession.
ALLEN: He was a fucking drug pusher!
ROSE: Where's your intellectual integrity, Allen? Where's your evidence?
ALLEN: Why did Wells lie about not having any business interests?
ROSE: There could be lots of reasons. It might even be true.
ALLEN: How could it be true? Here it is—Milton Imports registered in Queensland. Directors: Michael Wells and Graham White.
ROSE: You don't have to prove your identity when you register as a director.
ALLEN: What? Someone wanted to set him up? Who?
ROSE: The most likely candidate is obviously you.
ALLEN: Me! You don't think—
ROSE: Come off it, Allen. Your running battles with one another have provided half the political news for the last twelve months.

A slight pause.

ALLEN: Is that why you've been sleeping with me?
ROSE: I haven't been sleeping with you. We've been fucking.

A metal shearing noise.

ALLEN: Have you been able to find out anything useful?
ROSE: Don't play the innocent, Allen: you're prepared to use power that way.
ALLEN: What power?
ROSE: Do you expect me to believe you didn't intend to use me?
ALLEN: I didn't come to you with a story about Milton Imports! Is that why—?
ROSE: You told me where it was registered and now, on the flimsiest evidence, you want me to believe Michael Wells is involved in the drug trade. Don't you realise this could bring down the government?
ALLEN: I didn't send that balance sheet to you!
ROSE: Why are you so convinced of Wells' guilt?
ALLEN: I never intended to use you and I haven't!
ROSE: So you love me!
ALLEN: Yes!
ROSE: [*distressed*] No! I don't want your love!
ALLEN: Why did you come to me that day?
ROSE: Say it; say, 'I love you'.

Pause. She bursts into tears. A slight pause.

I'm glad of everything that's happened.

A slight pause.

ALLEN: What is it between us?
ROSE: You know. And that's exactly what I want.
ALLEN: I want to be able to love you.
ROSE: Then why do you whisper 'cunt' to me? Why do you scratch your fingers along my scars? Why the hate in your eyes as I come?
ALLEN: What's burnt your soul?
ROSE: The same thing that's burning yours. All that exists is power.
ALLEN: Love exists! We could love!
ROSE: So you love me, you want me, you don't feel real without me and so you fuck me and feel the horror in your heart and you fuck me harder because you love that guilt and pain because they're the only things you can feel—
ALLEN: What's left of your feeling? To be with a man you hate so you can act out a fantasy of power?

ACT THREE

ROSE: Show me I'm wrong, Allen, show me you're more than a petty powermonger trying to escape himself.
ALLEN: I don't need you.
ROSE: But you want me. I know you, Allen. I know the circles of your hate.
ALLEN: All you know is yourself.
ROSE: I want to be touched just once with affection.
ALLEN: You won't let me touch you!
ROSE: Why didn't you tell your wife you love me? What's love that's ashamed of itself?
ALLEN: My wife's got nothing to do with it.
ROSE: This world is perfect. There's nothing I want to change.
ALLEN: Listen to me! I love you.
ROSE: Liar!

The lights change.

SCENE FIVE

The steel mill gates. Afternoon.

The shift whistle blows. BRUCE *is handing out leaflets to* MEN *leaving the works. One of them pauses.*

MAN: What are you up to, son?

   BRUCE *and* DOUG *recognise each other.*

BRUCE: It's time we had a change.

   The MEN *stop momentarily to see* DOUG*'s reaction.* DOUG *approaches* BRUCE; BRUCE *hands him a leaflet.* DOUG *takes it and briefly looks at it; he looks at* BRUCE.

DOUG: You can come home to pack your gear.

   DOUG *walks off past the others, screwing the leaflet up and throwing it down. A slight pause;* BRUCE *continues to hand out leaflets. The lights change.*

SCENE SIX

The institute. Afternoon.
ALLEN *is on the phone.* ROSE *stands at a distance, watching him.*

ALLEN: [*into the phone*] Anything you can get on him, Max: convictions, charges… No—I don't know anyone in the Police Department. Will it be hard?… It's really important, I wouldn't ask if it wasn't… I know it's illegal… Look, we might not have another chance… Those bastards do it, why can't we?— Okay, thanks… As soon as you find out… Sure. See you.

    ALLEN *hangs up and sees* ROSE. *Pause.*

ROSE: Nothing hurts you.
ALLEN: You haven't tried hard enough yet.

    She begins to take off her blouse.

ROSE: Do you want me to try harder?
ALLEN: If it makes you feel real.
ROSE: I love you.

    The lights change.

SCENE SEVEN

Allen and Louise's house. Night.

LOUISE *has just entered.* ALLEN *has his back to her. The chess set is in front of him.*

LOUISE: Allen—love…
ALLEN: I don't want to know! I don't want to know where you've been, who you've been with, what you've been doing!

    Pause.

LOUISE: We're not the same.
ALLEN: Where were you?
LOUISE: You're the one who's mad.
ALLEN: I'm the one who's never at home—I'm the one—!
LOUISE: There was someone I needed to talk to.
ALLEN: I was here alone if you wanted to talk.
LOUISE: You're alone because you want to be.
ALLEN: I'm listening but I'm not hearing anything. Why don't you say what you mean?
LOUISE: What is it you think I'm not saying?
ALLEN: That we're finished. That our relationship is empty and you want to end it.

ACT THREE

LOUISE: If it's empty, why don't you want to end it?
>   *Pause.*

ALLEN: No! You think! You touch me!
>   *Pause.*

LOUISE: Touch me…
ALLEN: That night—the first night we met. That was the first time I was happy.
LOUISE: What do you want?
ALLEN: I want you to be what you are. My wife.
LOUISE: I don't need to be a wife to know who I am!
ALLEN: Who are you? What defines you?
LOUISE: I'm Louise Kraus! I have a name and a job! A life and a reality!
ALLEN: Keep going. What other tags? What other conceits?
LOUISE: What? Love? Loyalty? Honour? Those conceits?
ALLEN: Which love? The love of animals that lie down together?!
LOUISE: The love of comrades and socialism!
ALLEN: Where are they? Where in the length and breadth of this country is there any hope? In Ramon's dreams of a glorious democracy? In your feeble attempts to patch up the damage of broken homes?
LOUISE: Yes! And in the Unemployed Workers' Union! In the workers' occupations! There's a demonstration next week: what are you doing to help it succeed?
ALLEN: It'll fail no matter what I do.
LOUISE: What are you talking about?
ALLEN: It's perfect: capitalism constructs us in its own image. The law of competition becomes the central dynamic of personal relationships.
LOUISE: Why did you try to commit suicide, Allen?
ALLEN: You'll never understand me.
LOUISE: What threat do I pose to you?
ALLEN: I want somewhere to stand that's not moving!
LOUISE: Why did you want to be a priest?
ALLEN: I don't want this!
LOUISE: You gave up believing in God but couldn't give up the lie of Absolute Truth!
ALLEN: I need you, Louise.
LOUISE: You can't control me. That's why I'm a threat.

ALLEN: We're alone! We can't even talk to one another.
LOUISE: [*crying*] What happened to your hope, to your humanity?
ALLEN: [*crying*] When the whole world is slipping into misery and suffering—when you can't walk down the street without seeing the deformities we're being turned into. You want me to do what no-one else can do—and hold onto my humanity?
LOUISE: It's more important now than at any other time.
ALLEN: How? How? How can we be human when the poor cover themselves with cardboard boxes in the back alleys to keep warm? What kind of dignity can you maintain when you walk past people looking for food in garbage bins? Where in your soul can you exercise pride when twelve-year-olds are prostituting themselves to stay alive? Where are the humans that can live with that?
LOUISE: The humans struggling to change it.
ALLEN: We're the corpses of hope.
LOUISE: We're alive.
ALLEN: We're monsters, like them! There's nothing we can do!
LOUISE: We're free!
ALLEN: I've got a lover, Louise.

A slight pause.

LOUISE: What?
ALLEN: There's nothing in marriage worth having.
LOUISE: [*low*] No…
ALLEN: Are feminists the only ones allowed to take—?
LOUISE: Who is she?
ALLEN: Rose Draper, the journalist. She's got an interesting perspective—
LOUISE: No.
ALLEN: —on how a woman can effectively use her intelligence—
LOUISE: No! No!
ALLEN: Perhaps the four of us could get together. Is that what you mean about bringing sexuality into the public sphere?
LOUISE: Don't you have any pride?
ALLEN: You ask me that? When you're conducting an open affair with a woman I work with? What pride could I have?!
LOUISE: I'm not! I couldn't…
ALLEN: What do you mean you couldn't?! You are!
LOUISE: I was lying!

ALLEN: What?
LOUISE: I was lying! I was lying! We had one bad fuck! I was so guilty I threw up for two days after!
ALLEN: No! Why? Why did you lie to me?
LOUISE: Our whole relationship is a lie! Tell me it isn't true!
ALLEN: I can't believe it. Where would you go when you said you were seeing her?
LOUISE: To the movies. I'd walk around. I'd do the things I wanted to do with you.
ALLEN: It's bizarre. You're lying.
LOUISE: What are you turning into?
ALLEN: What am I turning into?
LOUISE: I need you, Allen!
ALLEN: 'S this what you wanted?
LOUISE: All I want is to chronicle the last screams of a dying world.

The lights change.

SCENE EIGHT

Doug's house. Night.

DOUG, EILEEN *and* BRUCE.

DOUG: Not in this house! Not in my home!
EILEEN: Where will he go?
DOUG: Keep out of it, Eileen.
EILEEN: How can I, when you're tearing the family apart?!
DOUG: Don't I have any authority left in my own house?
BRUCE: Who's got any authority when the company controls everything we do?
EILEEN: Don't provoke him, Bruce.
DOUG: They don't control me.
BRUCE: Everything we do—whether we can even live in this house—depends on them.
DOUG: I'm your father!
BRUCE: You're still a worker depending on them for a job.
DOUG: Who are you to tell me what I am?!
EILEEN: He didn't mean it, Doug!
BRUCE: I do! You're a worker! We both are!

DOUG: I'm a man and a man stands on his own legs. I'm not dependent on anyone.
BRUCE: What happens if you get the sack tomorrow?
DOUG: I'll get another job.
BRUCE: There's no other jobs!
DOUG: If I had to walk to the other side of the country, I'd get work.
BRUCE: You're too old, Dad.
EILEEN: Am I no-one in this house?
DOUG: I'm not too old to have some pride.
BRUCE: What pride?
DOUG: Knowing I'm a free man and my bread comes from my own labour.
EILEEN: I can't listen to this. Not again.
DOUG: Look at what you're doing to your mother.
BRUCE: We're not free!
EILEEN: It's you, Doug. One after another you rejected our sons because they opposed you.
DOUG: I fought for our freedom and your brother Francis died for it.
BRUCE: He didn't die for anything!
EILEEN: Bruce!
BRUCE: He died tryin' to live up to your ideas of what a man should be.
DOUG: He died fighting communism and you're trying to help them win!
BRUCE: That's what you said to Allen, wasn't it?
DOUG: No!
EILEEN: What?
BRUCE: You made him feel like he killed Frank himself. You made us all feel guilty for even standing up for you.
DOUG: Frank knew how to respect his father.
BRUCE: The only reason he joined the army was to prove to you he was a man. You killed him yourself!
DOUG: I loved my son! My only son.
BRUCE: You sent him out of the house! Just like you sent Allen before.
DOUG: I sent him out because he needed to pull himself together and he did. He died a man.
BRUCE: He was two years younger than I am now. He didn't know where he was or what he was doing.
EILEEN: He's dead, Doug. Why? He was a boy!
DOUG: [*upset*] Because he did his duty!

ACT THREE

BRUCE: Who to? To you! You didn't know a thing about that place or that war, but you sent him. Allen was right. It's on the TV. They were just people fighting for their freedom.
DOUG: Allen doesn't believe that anymore.
EILEEN: It was you, Doug. You pushing him, making them compete against each other, because you were always frightened you weren't a man yourself!
DOUG: I am a man! No-one's ever stood over me.
BRUCE: They stand over you every time you walk through those gates.
DOUG: You can't let them. You've got to fight 'em. You can't lose your self-respect.
BRUCE: That's what I'm fighting for!
EILEEN: Why are men always fighting? Why can't you live with yourselves the way you are?
DOUG: You fight because if you don't they'll grind the soul out of you.
EILEEN: How? Tell me why this is happening.
DOUG: By making you work in a hellhole for forty years where you got no say and all they want is your hands and eyes for as long as they can use 'em! By treating you like one of their machines they can pick up and put down wherever they like until your last bit of will and self-respect is wrung out of you and you're like a ghost that wanders around the place waiting to be told what to do. You have to fight every minute of the day to hold on to what's left of your humanity and if you don't you might as well be dead.
BRUCE: You can't fight by yourself.
DOUG: You can't trust anybody else.
EILEEN: What's the point of living if you can't trust anyone?
DOUG: To show 'em you can. To show 'em you're better than them!
EILEEN: What about me? Are you better than me?
BRUCE: You don't care about anyone. About Jim Mackie or anybody. You just want 'em to see how strong you are.
DOUG: I want 'em to see that a man can live!
BRUCE: I'm not gonna live like that.
DOUG: Like a man!
BRUCE: Like a slave. Obeying orders and pretendin' you're in control of your life 'cause you're better than the blokes who give 'em. That's nothin'. You're no different to anyone else there.

DOUG: This is my home! And in my home no-one tells me what to do or what I am.
EILEEN: It's my home, too and I won't let you destroy it.
DOUG: You're my wife and you'll do what I say!
EILEEN: I've done what you've said. For forty years I've done it. I won't see this happen again, Doug. I won't let you break another son of mine.
DOUG: The son obeys the father!
EILEEN: Only if he respects him.
DOUG: My sons respect me!
EILEEN: They're frightened of you! That's not respect.
DOUG: They respect me! If Allen's frightened of me why does he come here?
BRUCE: Because you made him guilty.
DOUG: Shut your mouth!
BRUCE: I heard what you said to him at the cemetery.
EILEEN: What?
DOUG: I didn't mean it!
BRUCE: Have you ever told him? Have you ever apologised?
EILEEN: What did he say?
BRUCE: That Allen put Frank in the grave. That he spat on his father and his family. That there was no love left between them.
EILEEN: You didn't!
DOUG: I was out of my mind!
EILEEN: How could you say that?!
DOUG: I was putting my son in the ground! I was mad with grief.
EILEEN: You did that at his graveside? You used his corpse against your own son?
BRUCE: And that's why he comes back every week looking for your forgiveness and you never said anything to him again because you had what you wanted: you had him kneeling before you!
DOUG: Shut up!
BRUCE: So you can take him aside and tell him how to conduct his marriage, how to treat his wife, how to lay down the law, how to be a man like you—and all the while you're king of the castle.
EILEEN: No! No!
DOUG: No more!

BRUCE: But you won't do it to me. I won't kneel in front of you.
DOUG: Get out of my house. You're no son of mine!
EILEEN: Stop!
BRUCE: If I have to lie and flatter to be your son, you're not my father. You're not even a man.
DOUG: Get out! Get out! I never want to see you again!
EILEEN: Why—?
DOUG: You were never born! You never existed! I don't know you! You're not my son!
EILEEN: Why?

The lights change.

SCENE NINE

Wells' office. Night.

CAREW *is with* WELLS.

WELLS: You've done nothing. Why?
CAREW: Sometimes there's nothing you can do.
WELLS: What are you here for, then?
CAREW: Your faith in my ability is gratifying, Mike, but I'm just stating a fact.
WELLS: Listen, son, this is where you start earning your keep: if you don't stop them, I'm sure there'll be more people than me you'll have to answer to.
CAREW: I think you're operating under a severe misunderstanding, Mike.
WELLS: I understand the left is poised to take control and you seem unwilling or unable to do anything about it.
CAREW: Your little chat with Fitzgerald didn't pay off, eh?
WELLS: What do you mean?
CAREW: You're losing your grip, Mike: five years ago you could've wrapped him up and made him a gift to State Conference. When did it all start getting away from you?
WELLS: Are you working for the embassy or not!
CAREW: No, I'm not. I'm a health and safety officer working for you.
WELLS: I want a straight answer out of you.
CAREW: Did you employ me thinking I was an American agent?

A slight pause.

WELLS: I'm the only one you can trust. Can't you see that?

CAREW: It did surprise me you were prepared to offer him a federal seat.

WELLS: How do you know that?

CAREW: It's very hard to keep secrets, Mike. There's the smell of death about you now—

WELLS: He couldn't have done anything in parliament!

CAREW: You look desperate. You don't trust me.

WELLS: You're selling me down the river, you prick. Who's going to replace me? Fitzgerald? Is he in your pocket now?

CAREW: I'd never have described our relationship in those terms, Mike.

WELLS: Who then? Why?

CAREW: You've lost control. You've let personal emotions get in the way. You couldn't even overcome your hatred of Fitzgerald to save yourself. It's bad form, Mike. I'm sorry.

WELLS: You'll be sorrier with me out of the way; Fitzgerald's cooking up a storm. It's not just him, it's everyone behind him—they'll be flooding Conference with socialist resolutions to break the American alliance. They'll be preselecting candidates for parliament. It'll be a disaster.

CAREW: Could you have stopped them? You wanted me to do everything because you don't have a power base anymore.

WELLS: I've got more power than you think.

CAREW: No, you don't. You let it slip away. All you've got are bullyboy tactics and empty threats.

A slight pause.

WELLS: What are you going to do?

CAREW: That's none of your concern anymore.

WELLS: Do you think I'm going to go without a fight? I've got shit on every politician in this country. Who's rootin' who, who's paying who off. If you want a political crisis, I can give it to you.

CAREW: Is that right? I'm sorry to hear it. There's a nasty rumour going round that you and Graham White were running drugs together.

WELLS: It was you. I should've guessed Fitzgerald couldn't come up with it by himself.

CAREW: You shouldn't take things so personally.

WELLS: Get out. I'll expose you. I'll crush you.
CAREW: Expose me as what? An American intelligence agent who's run your errands? You'd be laughed out of court.
WELLS: Get out!
CAREW: Take a last look, Wells. Like I said: no-one's indispensable.
WELLS: Get out!

The lights change.

SCENE TEN

The institute. Night.

ALLEN *is on the phone.* BOB *enters with a folder.*

ALLEN: [*into the phone*] I want Jane out of this joint as much as you do... Sure I'll vote with you... Sure: anyone you want... The sooner the better... Terrific—
BOB: G'day, comrade.
ALLEN: See you later.

He hangs up.

[*To* BOB] What brings you to this neck of the woods? It couldn't be that you want a loan.
BOB: I thought it was about time I collected.
ALLEN: You're too early. Payday's not till the end of the revolution.
BOB: We were going to have a drink.
ALLEN: I don't have time.
BOB: I phoned you, remember?
ALLEN: I remember, but I said I don't have time.
BOB: What's the matter?

A slight pause.

The stocks in social progress taken a dive?
ALLEN: Don't you understand English? I said I'm busy. What do you want?

A slight pause.

BOB: I've got something... I thought you might be able to use...
ALLEN: [*taking the folder*] Did it land anonymously on your desk one morning?

BOB: Michael Wells gave it to me. It's an American plan for the takeover of Austeel.

ALLEN: So what?

A slight pause.

BOB: What? I thought…

ALLEN: Everyone knew it was coming. The Yanks or the Japs: someone was going to take it over.

BOB: [*faltering*] But it's wrong.

ALLEN: Why?

BOB: I don't get it, Allen, you don't— Here's a definite plan to take over the major manufacturing base of the whole country!

ALLEN: The cunts have let the rest of the country go down the drain. Why not the steel industry?

BOB: [*uncertain*] You're joking…

ALLEN: Why bring it to me? What do you think I can do about it? Why not show it around to all your fucking bank mates? All the influential economists you know who've got so much commitment to this country.

A slight pause.

BOB: Allen…?

A slight pause.

ALLEN: I'm not interested, Bob. If you want to do something, go ahead and do it.

BOB: What could I do?

A slight pause.

ALLEN: Sure, I know…

BOB: I've got my job: I'm putting myself on the line just bringing it to you.

ALLEN: They've really got you fucked, haven't they?

BOB: What can I do?

ALLEN: Nothing. You're right. There's nothing you can do.

BOB: I brought it to you.

ALLEN: I don't want it.

BOB: They're going to close the place down, Allen. They'll import everything. We won't have a manufacturing sector left.

ALLEN: That's capitalism.

The lights change.

SCENE ELEVEN

Allen and Louise's house. Night.

A shutter is banging in the wind. ALLEN *and* RAMON *are in the lounge room finishing a meal.*

RAMON: There'll be a caucus of left unions immediately after the election. We'll call for a spill and put our candidates forward.

The phone rings. ALLEN *goes to answer it.* LOUISE *enters to take the plates away. Spotlight on* ALLEN.

ALLEN: [*into the phone*] Hello… Max.
RAMON: [*to* LOUISE] The food was very good, Louise.
LOUISE: Thank you.
RAMON: Are you going to march with your union at the demonstration?
LOUISE: No.
RAMON: You should march with the union, comrade: the women might be noisy, but the workers have the power.
LOUISE: I'm not marching at all.

A slight pause.

RAMON: Why not? Are you sick?
LOUISE: No.

A slight pause.

RAMON: Then why?
LOUISE: I've got other things to do.
RAMON: But it'll be great! There'll be thousands of people.
LOUISE: [*going to the window*] One more won't make any difference.
RAMON: Every one makes the difference!
LOUISE: [*looking out the window*] The storm is starting.
RAMON: It's very strange. Where does all the dust come from?
LOUISE: The drought's lasted too long. The country is blowing away.
ALLEN: [*into the phone*] Good.

ALLEN *hangs up.* LOUISE *turns.*

LOUISE: How's Maria, Ramon?

RAMON: Good. Her back is better.
LOUISE: You should have brought her over.
RAMON: She had to look after the kids. Maybe another time.
LOUISE: Maybe.

>   ALLEN *rejoins them.*

ALLEN: I've got him.

>   LOUISE *exits with the dishes.*

RAMON: Who?
ALLEN: Wells. He's finished. The Police Department had Graham White under surveillance for six months. He was into drug pushing, gun running, the works. And Wells had the investigation stopped.
RAMON: It doesn't matter: we're going to win the election.
ALLEN: I'm going to destroy him!
RAMON: What?
ALLEN: I'll finish him for good. There'll be nothing left when I get through with him.
RAMON: What are you talking about? He's finished.
ALLEN: He's not finished till he's in jail with every other drug pusher and murderer in this state.
RAMON: Our aim was to politically eliminate him.
ALLEN: And let him hang around to organise an opposition?
RAMON: We don't have anything to fear from oppositions as long as we do what the workers want.
ALLEN: I'm through with rhetoric, Ramon!
RAMON: Rhetoric?
ALLEN: I want Wells dead!
RAMON: Allen?
ALLEN: The fuckin' cunt…
RAMON: What is it in your country that feeds on hate!
ALLEN: How can't you hate?!
RAMON: Because it kills your heart. My father and my brother were tortured and killed by the fascists in seventy-three. But if all that was left of me was hate it would be best for everyone for me to be in the grave! You have no right to say these things, because you don't know!
ALLEN: I know what I've become.
RAMON: You choose what you become, mate.

ACT THREE

ALLEN: Yes, I chose, Ramon. I chose to deal with Palmer.
RAMON: We dealt with Palmer because there was no other way!
ALLEN: Then I embraced the inevitable, Ramon. I made a pact with the devil.
RAMON: Are you a child?
ALLEN: We've been childish to think we could ever change anything.
RAMON: We're changing it!
ALLEN: And it's changing us!
RAMON: Yes! We're growing. The people are feeling their power for the first time. Allen—
ALLEN: The people are corrupt—
RAMON: No!
ALLEN: —they've lived too long on the crumbs of crime and genocide; they've learnt too well to obey their masters and deliver up their children! They have no shame, no pride, no vision. They're dead!
RAMON: Are you nuts? You talk like a fuckin' fascist. Don't you understand all your power comes from the workers?
ALLEN: My power comes from myself.
RAMON: By yourself you're nothing, an insect. We'll brush you aside as easily as Wells. You're no-one.
ALLEN: Get out of my house.
RAMON: What?
ALLEN: Get out of my house!
RAMON: You cut my soul, Allen. Of anyone, I trusted you the most.
ALLEN: You should never trust anyone.

The lights change.

SCENE TWELVE

The Rank and File Co-ordinating Centre. Day.

RAMON, BRUCE *and other* WORKERS. ROBIN *is reading* Seven Poor Men of Sydney. BRUCE *is on the phone. He hangs up.*

BRUCE: [*to* RAMON] Tony rang from Austeel and said it's still iffy. I think if we went out tomorrow: there's part of the plant that's really dangerous since the retrenchments…

The phone rings.

… I think we can clinch it.

RAMON: Can't you do it yourself?
BRUCE: A lot of 'em still think they're my uncle.
MARGIE: Phone, Ramon.
RAMON: [*to* BRUCE *as he exits*] I have to talk to you in a minute.

> RAMON *is gone. A slight pause.*

BRUCE: [*tiredly*] Christ. [*To* ROBIN] How come you're the only one not doing any work?
ROBIN: Because I've been here organising the unemployed demo since six o'clock this morning, smart-arse.
BRUCE: How's it going?
ROBIN: It's going to be a beauty.
BRUCE: You must be buggered. Why don't you go home?
ROBIN: I'm obviously waiting for some rising trade union bureaucrat to ask me out for a Chinese meal.
BRUCE: My thoughts exactly.
ROBIN: Who did you have in mind?
BRUCE: Harry Tanner should be stumbling in from the pub in a minute.
ROBIN: No, he's mine.
BRUCE: You like a beer gut between you and your patron?
ROBIN: I like taking my time getting to know someone.
BRUCE: Stuff that. Helen Caldicott says we've only got till December before they blow the joint up.
ROBIN: [*holding up her book*] Have you ever read this?
BRUCE: No. What is it?
ROBIN: Christina Stead: *Seven Poor Men of Sydney*.
BRUCE: What's it about?
ROBIN: How people survive.
BRUCE: How do they?

> RAMON *enters.*

RAMON: Bruce, I have to talk to you.

> *A slight pause.*

BRUCE: [*to* ROBIN] I'll see you later on.
ROBIN: Yeah. Maybe over noodles.

> *A slight pause;* BRUCE *hesitates.*

BRUCE: What's up?

ACT THREE 93

RAMON: You have to help your brother.
BRUCE: Why? What's happened?
> *The lights change.*

SCENE THIRTEEN

The institute. Night.

ALLEN *is on the phone.*

ALLEN: [*into the phone*] I need those branches for tomorrow night: we have to be as solid as we can… Stack them if you have to. Forge the fucking membership cards, I don't care! I'm going to do Wells tomorrow night and I'm going to be secretary!
BRUCE: [*off*] Allen…
> ALLEN *slams down the phone in shock.*

Allen…
> *A slight pause.*

ALLEN: Yes.
BRUCE: [*entering*] It's me, Bruce… Can I come in?
ALLEN: Sure.
> *A slight pause.*

BRUCE: Never been here before. Had a bit of trouble finding it.
ALLEN: I meant to get in touch. Mum gave me your address.
BRUCE: I been working over the Rank and File for the last few days.
ALLEN: Have you?
BRUCE: Looks like we're in, eh mate?
> *Pause.*

Who were you talking to on the phone?
> ALLEN *stands abruptly.*

ALLEN: Nobody. You feel like going to the pub?
BRUCE: I come over to talk… Ramon said you 'n' him had a blue.
ALLEN: What did he tell you?
BRUCE: He didn't tell me nothin'— What's the trouble?
ALLEN: Disagreement.
BRUCE: Yeah, he's a cantankerous bastard, isn't he?

ALLEN: He's a hero of the working class.
BRUCE: Eh?
ALLEN: When the coup happened, he fought at the university with the students. He was wounded and captured and tortured for three weeks.

> *A slight pause.*

BRUCE: I didn't know. So what did you fight about?

> *Pause.*

ALLEN: There were thirty-six thousand people murdered, Bruce: the best militants, the political leaders. Pinochet said he'd be prepared to kill two hundred thousand to save Chile from Marxism.

> *A slight pause.*

BRUCE: What are you saying?
ALLEN: Do you want the same thing to happen here?
BRUCE: How could it? This is a democracy.
ALLEN: So was Chile.
BRUCE: I can't see what you're getting at.
ALLEN: It doesn't matter.
BRUCE: Are you saying because there might be a coup, we shouldn't try to change things?
ALLEN: I'm saying the only way you can change things is by revolution.
BRUCE: How you going to make a revolution in Australia? Geez, you can see Dad in that one, can't ya?

> *Pause.*

He kicked me out of the house; ya know that, don't ya?
ALLEN: You shouldn't have answered back.
BRUCE: Why not? He's wrong.

> *A slight pause.*

ALLEN: You'll regret it.
BRUCE: It was time I left, anyhow. I'm finished at the steel mill now.
ALLEN: They sack you?
BRUCE: Yeah. The foreman told me I'd never work in the metal industry again. Is that what the fight was about? You tell Ramon he was up shit creek?
ALLEN: The world's more complicated than you think.

ACT THREE

BRUCE: What are you doing, then? Why are we trying to win this election?

Pause.

I heard what Dad said to you at Frank's funeral…
ALLEN: What?
BRUCE: 'Bout you killing him. It was a bastard act.
ALLEN: You don't understand, do you?
BRUCE: What?
ALLEN: He's not just a man. He's our father!
BRUCE: So what? Does that give him the right—?
ALLEN: Yes! The right! The right to do anything! The right over life and death!
BRUCE: Are you kidding?
ALLEN: That's the only way our lives can have meaning!
BRUCE: Have you gone nuts? Fucking hell—
ALLEN: Why did Ramon send you over?
BRUCE: I came for a talk.
ALLEN: Don't lie to me, Bruce: what did he say?
BRUCE: He said you needed help.
ALLEN: I don't need anything!

A slight pause.

BRUCE: You know, I watched you grow up. All the blues you had with Dad— He was a pig to you.
ALLEN: Don't, Bruce— You think you know, but you don't. You don't even know you're alive.
BRUCE: I know I wouldn't have tried to commit suicide because I was too frightened to tell Dad I didn't believe in God anymore!
ALLEN: I never believed! Can you understand that? I became a priest because I wanted to believe!
BRUCE: [*confused*] You wanted to—?
ALLEN: What's going to happen when he dies, Bruce?
BRUCE: Slow down—
ALLEN: How are you going to live the rest of your life knowing he never loved you?
BRUCE: He loves us!
ALLEN: He doesn't know us! The only way we can live with him is by lying!

BRUCE: I never lied to him!
ALLEN: And he sent you out of the house cursing you!
BRUCE: If he's a man, he'll admit he was wrong and bring me home!
ALLEN: One night I sat with my legs over the edge. I saw the empty passion, the madness!
BRUCE: Is that what you're frightened of? His rejection?
ALLEN: His rejection? You think I care about that? He's pathetic!
BRUCE: What are you saying? I can't—
ALLEN: Can you imagine what I felt like when he told me about—when he accused me of Frank's death? To see him degrade himself that way and know he was my father!
BRUCE: I thought—
ALLEN: How much of the phone call did you hear?
BRUCE: Not much. And I didn't believe what I did.
ALLEN: We've got to get rid of Wells, Bruce.
BRUCE: We're going to. We're going to win the election.
ALLEN: That's not enough.
BRUCE: Why not?
ALLEN: Trust me.
BRUCE: You were the one who taught me the importance of integrity—
ALLEN: Who are you to judge me!
BRUCE: I'm not judging you. I'm your brother.
ALLEN: Then forget what you heard.
BRUCE: No. I won't let you do that. We're supposed to have some kind of principles.
ALLEN: We don't have any principles.
BRUCE: What are you talking about? 'Course we got fucking principles. We're not the same as them.
ALLEN: You don't think so? Did Ramon tell you the deal I had to make with Charlie Palmer to keep us in the party?

A slight pause.

BRUCE: What deal?
ALLEN: That any party or criminal investigations against him had to be stopped. Do you know what that means, Bruce? That we'll be protecting him while he's pumping heroin into this state and putting fifteen-year-olds into his brothels for his elite fucking clientele—

ACT THREE

BRUCE: No.
ALLEN: Capitalism's perfect, Bruce: there's no way you can overthrow it.
BRUCE: You wouldn't do that!
ALLEN: I did it. It was my socialist duty. To celebrate our agreement, Palmer invited me to his best whorehouse and take any woman I liked. As many as I wanted! Nothing's too good for comrade Fitzgerald!
BRUCE: Why? There must have been a reason.
ALLEN: To get rid of Wells.
BRUCE: That's not what this is about.
ALLEN: What's it about, Bruce? Does it matter?
BRUCE: Yes! It matters what sort of men we are!
ALLEN: We're men like them!
BRUCE: So what happened? Did you go to the brothel with him?
ALLEN: Yes.
BRUCE: I don't believe—
ALLEN: I wanted it, Bruce. I wanted to feel everything—
BRUCE: [*over him*] You didn't! Tell me you're lying!
ALLEN: —that stinking deal meant! I wanted that horror—
BRUCE: [*over him*] Not you!
ALLEN: —that degradation!
BRUCE: How could you?!
ALLEN: Because if I was going to do it, I wanted it all. I'm lost, Bruce. Get out before I burn you.
BRUCE: Allen!
ALLEN: Don't look at me.
BRUCE: Why?
ALLEN: [*anguished*] It's as if I was knocked off balance and I've been falling ever since! That everything I do to try to regain myself only makes it worse… as if I want to destroy everything!
BRUCE: Do you?
ALLEN: I'm frightened I do. Stop me!
BRUCE: I'm here. Hold onto me.
ALLEN: I'm monstrous!
BRUCE: You're my brother!
ALLEN: Then shiver in fear.
BRUCE: Allen! Jesus Christ!
ALLEN: I'm damned! Get out!

BRUCE: There's forgiveness, Allen! Even for you!
ALLEN: Not for me. Not for any of us.

The lights change.

SCENE FOURTEEN

A room. Night.

WELLS *is on the phone.*

WELLS: [*into the phone*] I don't want him at that meeting tomorrow!… Yes, tonight!… I don't care what you do! And the other one: he's going out to Austeel tomorrow. Make sure he doesn't come back. Do you understand?… Ring me when you're finished.

He hangs up.

SCENE FIFTEEN

Allen's house. Night.

Four MEN, *armed with clubs, et cetera, are waiting for* ALLEN, *unseen. The sinister and violent content of this scene is all in the direction.* ALLEN *enters.*

ALLEN: Louise…

Pause. He moves forward.

Louise—are you home?… Who's there?

A MAN *lunges with a club.*

FIRST THUG: Cop one from Mike.

ALLEN *reacts quickly, knocking the club from the* MAN's *hand; it rattles across the floor.*

ALLEN: Cop this!
SECOND THUG: Look out!
THIRD THUG: Get him!

ALLEN *runs and picks up the club as the* OTHERS *move in.*

FIRST THUG: Where is he?
ALLEN: [*swinging the club*] Come on, ya cunts! I been waiting for you! I been fucking waiting for you!

ACT THREE

Screams, confusion erupts.

FOURTH THUG: He's mad!
ALLEN: I'll kill all of you! I'll kill the fuckin' lot of ya!

The lights change.

SCENE SIXTEEN

The steel mill. Day.

RAMON, BRUCE *and* OTHERS. *Loud factory noise.*

BRUCE: Since the retrenchments, it's not safe to work here: look at those wires. Why haven't they been repaired?

    RAMON *pulls* BRUCE *aside.*

RAMON: There's something funny here, comrade.
BRUCE: What?
RAMON: Do you trust all these men?
BRUCE: Why?
RAMON: They look as if they expect something.
BRUCE: I'll keep my eyes open.
RAMON: Surround us with men you know.

    All sound effects stop. The lights change.

SCENE SEVENTEEN

The institute. Day.

ALLEN *and* DOUG.

DOUG: You got nothing on your chest, have you, Allen?
ALLEN: No, Dad.
DOUG: We're mates, aren't we?
ALLEN: Yes, Dad.
DOUG: [*embracing him*] My son: the only one I've got left.

    The lights change.

SCENE EIGHTEEN

The steel mill. Day.

RAMON, BRUCE *and* OTHERS. *Loud factory noise.*

BRUCE: There should be five men here, not two. It's not safe.
FIRST WORKER: We can do it.
BRUCE: What happens if one of you has an accident? What can the other one do?
SECOND WORKER: 'Course he's fucking right! It's dangerous!
FIRST WORKER: You're just not used to it.
SECOND WORKER: You nearly got your arm caught the other day, you mug.

The lights change.

SCENE NINETEEN

A room. Day.

WELLS *is waiting impatiently for a phone call. Pause. The phone rings. The lights change.*

SCENE TWENTY

The factory. Day.

RAMON, BRUCE *and* OTHERS. *They are now in an obviously dangerous area.*

BRUCE: The handrail's rusted away! There aren't even any fucking harnesses here in case you fall!
RAMON: This is terrible! You men should not be here. What happens if you fall? You go straight into the metal! I would say to you, my friends, you must walk off the job immediately—

A MAN *runs towards* BRUCE *and* RAMON *standing precariously on the edge.* RAMON *sees him.*

[*To* BRUCE] Look out, comrade!

RAMON *tries to stop the* MAN *but is pushed off the edge into the molten metal. Confusion and horror. The* MAN *runs.*

BRUCE: Get him! Get the cunt! Get him!

The lights change.

SCENE TWENTY-ONE

An executive meeting. Night.

ALLEN *and* WELLS *are standing on the rostrum.*

ALLEN: I have absolute proof—
WELLS: They're lies!
CHAIR: Order!
ALLEN: —that, while secretary of this party, Michael Wells was financially involved with the drug trafficker Graham White. That he personally stopped the police investigation of White and has a continued involvement in the company through which the transactions were made. What sort of party are we? The party of ordinary Australians or the party of drug pushers and criminals? Michael Wells must go!

A slight pause.

CHAIR: Does the secretary wish to answer the charges?
WELLS: Comrades, everything you've heard is a complete lie! The party is under attack from both the left and the right. Both Fitzgerald and Sir Leslie Harris are prepared to smear the party with any deceit and falsehood. If we are to retain government we have to remain united!
VOICE: What about the charges?!
WELLS: They're lies put up by Fitzgerald and the CIA—

Laughter, boos.

Few of you realise the power the Americans have in this country!
VOICE: The charges!
WELLS: Let Fitzgerald tell you about his involvement in drugs!
VOICE: [*chanting*] The charges! The charges!
WELLS: I have nothing to answer! I'm innocent! It's a fabrication. I've been framed!
SECOND VOICE: [*chanting over the other*] Out! Out! Out!
WELLS: They're trying to get rid of me to destroy the party!
ALLEN: [*joining in*] Out! Out! Out! Out!
CHAIR: Order!
WELLS: I'm innocent!

The lights change.

SCENE TWENTY-TWO

Wells' office. Night.

ALLEN *and* WELLS. WELLS *is physically shrunken: his clothes are somehow too big for him. A slight pause.*

WELLS: Is this what you wanted?
ALLEN: A part.
WELLS: You're a puppet of the left.
ALLEN: I'm no-one's puppet.
WELLS: The party will split now, and the government will fall.
ALLEN: No it won't. I can keep the left under control.
WELLS: You think so?
ALLEN: Anything they get will have to come from me.
WELLS: [*beginning to laugh*] From you? From you! You fucking fool.

The phone rings.

ALLEN: Have you got any other words of wisdom before you go?
WELLS: I hope you rot in hell!
ALLEN: [*picking up the phone*] Piss off. [*Into the phone*] Hello… Rose.

WELLS exits.

My first phone call as secretary— [*Joking*] What do you want? An interview?… Your house? Sure—where do you live?

The lights change.

SCENE TWENTY-THREE

The Rank and File Co-ordinating Centre. Day.

BRUCE *and* ROBIN.

BRUCE: He's betrayed us! He's not going to back us up on anything!
ROBIN: What can we do?
BRUCE: I know what we can start off with.
ROBIN: What?
BRUCE: We'll occupy the party building at the demo.
ROBIN: They'll expel us if we do that.
BRUCE: Fuck 'em! What's the point in being in the fucking thing anyway?!
   We have to organise outside the party: the whole thing's fucked.

ACT THREE 103

ROBIN: He's your brother.
BRUCE: He's the enemy.

The lights change.

SCENE TWENTY-FOUR

Rose's bedroom. Night.

ALLEN *and* ROSE. *The wind bell tinkles. A slight pause.*

ALLEN: A wind bell. There was one the first time we met.
ROSE: Don't tell me you're getting sentimental.

A slight pause.

ALLEN: I've never been here before. I thought you wanted to keep yourself secret.
ROSE: Describe the room to me.
ALLEN: [*uncertain*] What?
ROSE: What's in it?
ALLEN: [*uneasy*] A vase… daffodils… curtains… a Picasso print—
ROSE: Is there anything in this room that reminds you of me?

A slight pause.

ALLEN: No.
ROSE: What do you think of me?
ALLEN: Why did you ask me here?
ROSE: [*producing a gun*] Have you ever seen a gun?
ALLEN: What do you want, Rose?
ROSE: You know I told you I'd been in El Salvador: that's where I got this. Does this remind you of me?
ALLEN: Yes.
ROSE: I had a boyfriend in Salvador, Allen. A young leftist. A warrior. He was like you, only much better, much stronger, much more passionate, much more guts. Do you know what I did?
ALLEN: What?
ROSE: I betrayed him and he was killed. He died loving me.
ALLEN: Why did you do that?
ROSE: Because I wanted a story.
ALLEN: Did you get it?

ROSE: Oh, yes, I got it. And lots of others. I was the best war correspondent there until I got shot.

ALLEN: Who shot you?

ROSE: Oh, all that was true. It was an accident. Lots of accidents happen in Salvador.

ALLEN: Why are you telling me now?

ROSE: Because I know you're interested in history.

ALLEN: What history?

ROSE: The history of my involvement with the Americans. I am working with the Americans, Allen. I've always told you the truth.

ALLEN: And your mission was to destroy me?

ROSE: Yes. And I've done that.

ALLEN: How?

ROSE: The material you used to overthrow Wells was a complete fabrication. It was a fabrication concocted by you. They've got you, Allen: it was all a lie.

Pause.

ALLEN: I'm glad. And sleeping with me—was that their idea, too?

ROSE: No, that was my own.

ALLEN: Why?

ROSE: I wanted to see you up close. I wanted to see how power possessed you. I've always been fascinated by power.

A slight pause.

ALLEN: Are you going to kill me?

ROSE: No. I want you to live.

ALLEN: Why?

ROSE: So you can be eaten alive by your torment.

A slight pause.

ALLEN: You won.

ROSE: Yes, I did. Now get out. I never want to see you again.

A slight pause. ALLEN *begins to exit.*

Allen…

He hesitates.

… I hoped you'd win.

ALLEN: How much did they pay you?
ROSE: Nothing. I did it for the love.
ALLEN: Don't go near the balcony: the drop's not big enough to kill you.

He exits. The lights change.

SCENE TWENTY-FIVE

Rose's bedroom. Night.

The Beatles' 'You Never Give Me Your Money' is playing. ROSE *walks quietly across the stage with a glass of wine. She puts the wine down and picks up the gun. She then walks to the balcony and shoots herself.*

SCENE TWENTY-SIX

Wells' office. Day.

Outside are the sounds of a demonstration and a WOMAN'S VOICE *delivering a speech. The speech and accompanying chants, et cetera, are heard over the following scenes.*

The speech does not contain the 'message' of the play and is merely the audio cue of the exterior action. The action of the scene takes place uninterruptedly over it. The last few lines of the speech, however, to which ALLEN *replies, 'Lies' (p.109), are important, and the volume should be brought up so the audience can hear the statements clearly.*

WOMAN: [*voice-over*] When the government lies to the people it has no right to govern! The people are its only mandate and power. They call on us now to defend them against the ruling class, when they've backed the ruling class against us since their election. When we demanded jobs they endorsed retrenchments; when we demanded an end to American bases they extended American control of our national life; when we demanded democratisation they became more secretive in their dealings with the bosses! But now it's their turn to listen to us! We won't defend the government, but we will defend our power. We'll smash Sir Leslie Harris or any other capitalist who stands in the way of the people! Instead of nationalisation we demand socialisation! Instead of wage cuts and unemployment we demand shorter working hours and a redistribution of wealth!

Instead of being told by bureaucrats what to do, we demand the government do what the people tells it!

ALLEN is looking at the TransOcean report. CAREW enters.

CAREW: They've filled the whole street. There's a possibility they're going to try to occupy.

ALLEN: Have you locked the doors?

CAREW: Yes, and the police are two deep in front, but I'm not sure if they can hold. There's hundreds out there.

ALLEN: Who are they?

CAREW: Unemployed, women's groups—the usual ratbags. We're photographing them at the moment— Your friend Bob Lang is out there.

ALLEN: He's not my friend. Invite a delegation in to see me—anyone except my brother.

CAREW goes to leave.

Oh, look: here's that TransOcean submission—it looks fine to me. Do you want to get it over to the Premier's Office?

CAREW takes the report.

Leave the window. I want to hear them.

As CAREW mimes opening a window, the level of offstage noises rises slightly. CAREW moves towards the door.

Is my car ready?

CAREW: It's waiting in the basement.

He exits. ALLEN listens to the speech.

WOMAN: [*voice-over*] The people want a just society where they can live in peace and happiness! They don't want to be part of a war machine on the edge of the holocaust!

BRUCE enters.

The people want freedom and democracy and a say in the decisions that affect them, not to be the factory and cannon fodder in the mindless pursuit of profit! Ramon Gris showed us the life of the revolutionary: of love and dedication, of passion and commitment. He showed us how to be human in the most inhuman world; how to have courage when everyone around is cowering.

ACT THREE

> *The sound continues over as previously.*

BRUCE: You made it.

> *A slight pause.*

ALLEN: Yes, I did.
BRUCE: Is that all you wanted: just to use us to get power?
ALLEN: One day you might understand.
BRUCE: What? That you betrayed us?
ALLEN: That the world is a perfect reflection of the human heart.
BRUCE: Not mine. Not Ramon's.
ALLEN: Yours, Ramon's, mine, Louise's.
BRUCE: Why did you do it?
ALLEN: Because I wanted it.
BRUCE: I loved you.
ALLEN: Do you want something, Bruce?
WOMAN: [*voice-over*] He showed us what life could be like: not alienated and distorted, but whole. He lived and died as a socialist to bring that world into being: where no person stands over another; where we can greet each other as equals; where men and women can live and work together without fear…

> *Sound over as before.*

BRUCE: The dust storm is coming: it'll cover you up.
ALLEN: You'll learn you can't win.
BRUCE: We're winning.
ALLEN: [*into the intercom*] Don—there's an intruder in my office.
BRUCE: I'll go. But I'll be back with the others.
ALLEN: If you do, you won't be the same.
BRUCE: No, I won't.

> BRUCE *exits.* ALLEN *wanders closer to the window.*

WOMAN: [*voice-over*] In a society not bowed before imperialism—
ALLEN: Lies.
VOICE: [*off*] Ramon Gris!
OTHERS: [*off*] Present!
WOMAN: [*voice-over*] In a society where human values can breathe—
ALLEN: Lies.
VOICES: [*off*] Occupy! Occupy! Occupy!

WOMAN: [*voice-over*] In a society of freedom and democracy we can build together and no-one can destroy.
ALLEN: Lies.
VOICE: [*off*] Smash in the door!
SECOND VOICE: [*off*] Smash the doors down!
WOMAN: [*voice-over*] By occupying this building, we reclaim the power that is ours!

The sound of a clash, doors being broken, et cetera, chanting.

ALLEN: You fools. Burn… burn… burn… burn—
BRUCE: [*off*] We're winning!
ALLEN: Burn!

All sound effects stop. A swift light change.

SCENE TWENTY-SEVEN

LOUISE *screaming. Blackout.*

THE END

Belvoir presents

THE BLIND GIANT IS DANCING

By **STEPHEN SEWELL**
Director **EAMON FLACK**

This production of The Blind Giant is Dancing *opened at Belvoir St Theatre on Wednesday 17 February 2016.*

Set & Costume Designer **DALE FERGUSON**
Lighting Designer **VERITY HAMPSON**
Composer & Sound Designer **STEVE TOULMIN**
Fight Choreographer **SCOTT WITT**
Stage Manager **MELANIE STANTON**
Assistant Stage Manager **GRACE NYE-BUTLER**

With
Mr Carew **MICHAEL DENKHA**
Ramon Gris **IVAN DONATO**
Bruce Fitzgerald **ANDREW HENRY**
Janice / Jane / Robin **EMMA JACKSON**
Doug Fitzgerald / Sir Leslie Harris **RUSSELL KIEFEL**
Eileen Fitzgerald **GENEVIEVE LEMON**
Michael Wells **GEOFF MORRELL**
Rose Draper **ZAHRA NEWMAN**
Allen Fitzgerald **DAN SPIELMAN**
Louise Kraus **YAEL STONE**
Bob Lang **BEN WOOD**

PHOTOGRAPHY Brett Boardman
DESIGN Alphabet Studio

Dan Spielman

WRITER'S NOTE

Stephen Sewell

When I wrote *The Blind Giant is Dancing* at the beginning of the eighties, in the Australia of Neville Wran and Joh Bjelke-Petersen, of Peter Baldwin's bashing in a bitter inter-factional fight and deep-seated corruption at all levels of Australian society, the country was at a watershed that would soon see the economic model that had grown out of the Second World War, and based on the idea of developing a strong manufacturing base behind a protective wall of tariffs and quotas, dismantled and abandoned in favour of the allegedly free markets being championed by President Ronald Reagan in what would ultimately be called the Neo-Conservative Revolution, whose dismal fruits we are enjoying today in a catastrophic collapse of international political and economic order.

But that was thirty years away – a whole generation – in the course of which Australia was completely transformed, with one of the major changes being the utter destruction of the working class that had served that very same manufacturing base, and had learnt how to defend itself through organisations such as Trade Unions and the different political parties, notably the Australian Labor Party and the Communist Party of Australia, with the ALP under Prime Minister Bob Hawke ironically being the party seeking to modernise Australian capitalism by enthusiastically embracing market theory, with ultimately devastating results. In the place of the once-organised working class we now have instead a mass of atomised workers, often simply referred to as 'contractors' without even minimal rights, serving in various functions the economy that has grown from the ruins of manufacturing, with mining, for example, as well as the service industries, construction, retailing, agriculture and the like now representing the main pillars of what prosperity the country enjoys. And beneath these workers, there is an even more harshly treated underclass of almost a million people on Temporary Work Visas, often suffering gross physical abuse and terrible exploitation, and whose plight it seems is totally beyond the ken of the responsible authorities to do anything about. As a result of these changes, inequality in Australia has surged, making it one of the most unequal countries in the OECD, with fourteen percent of people now living beneath the poverty line, and eighteen percent of children, and rising. Needless to say, we now also have more billionaires than ever before, and some might think this balances the picture.

But even though these things were in the future for the characters of the play, and the first audiences, they knew that momentous times were upon them that required their utmost attention, and what is exciting to me as a writer looking back at the beginning of my writing career, is how *alive* all these people now seem.

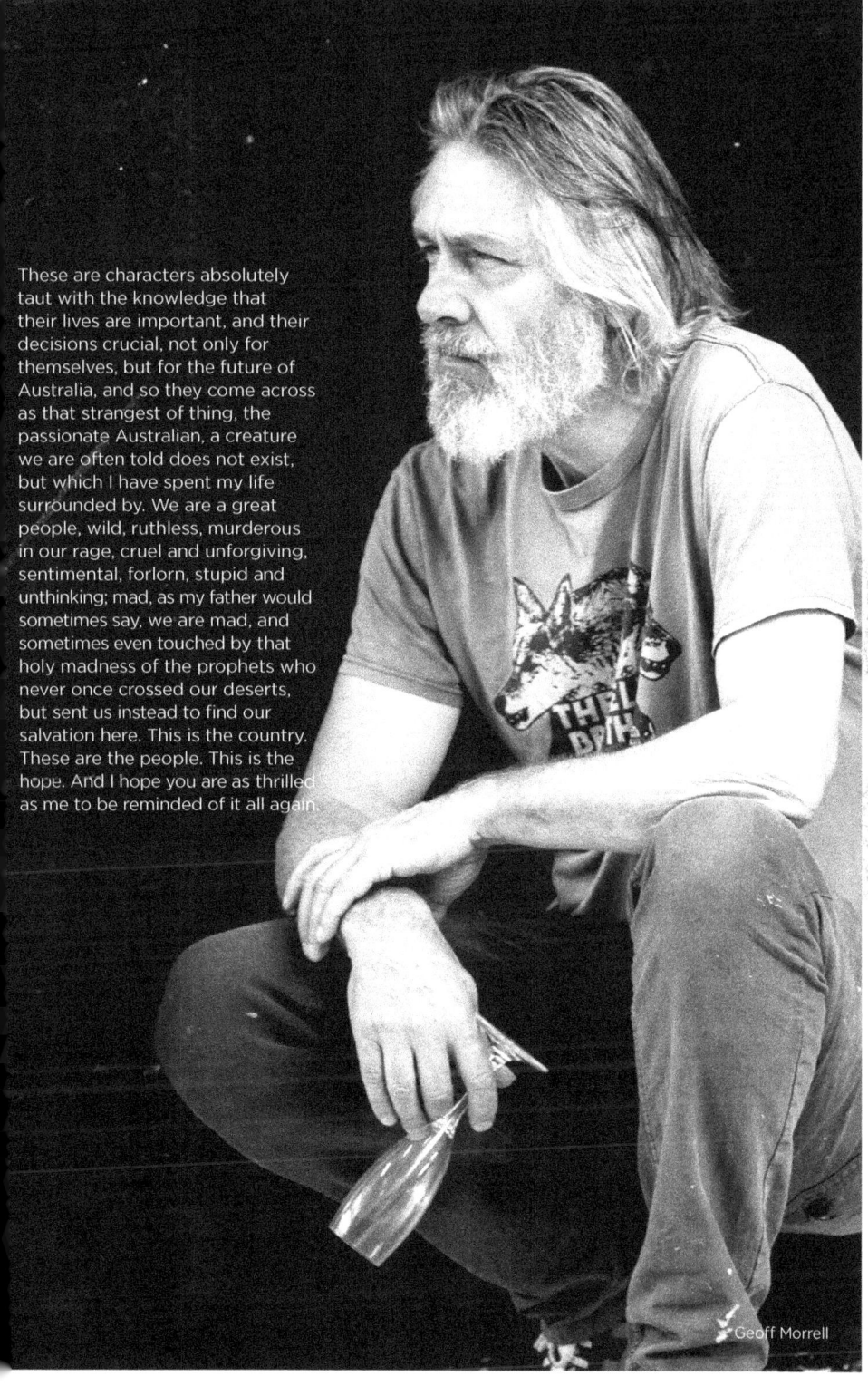

These are characters absolutely taut with the knowledge that their lives are important, and their decisions crucial, not only for themselves, but for the future of Australia, and so they come across as that strangest of thing, the passionate Australian, a creature we are often told does not exist, but which I have spent my life surrounded by. We are a great people, wild, ruthless, murderous in our rage, cruel and unforgiving, sentimental, forlorn, stupid and unthinking; mad, as my father would sometimes say, we are mad, and sometimes even touched by that holy madness of the prophets who never once crossed our deserts, but sent us instead to find our salvation here. This is the country. These are the people. This is the hope. And I hope you are as thrilled as me to be reminded of it all again.

Geoff Morrell

DIRECTOR'S NOTE

Eamon Flack

I've wanted to do this play, somehow or other, for a long time. When I was at drama school I wanted to play Allen Fitzgerald. His rage was something I knew well: the vicious desire to supercede your Catholic human shittiness, the guilty need to prove you still have moral compass – a need you pursue so desperately and demonstrably that you end up competing with your dead god by joining the ALP or becoming a theatre director… I never took the ALP seriously enough to join, and I never did get to play Allen Fitzgerald at drama school, but here I am the Artistic Director of Belvoir and it seems that I should get this great play out of my system at the outset.

The ranks of artists and politicians are filled with damaged goods, and I'm convinced that the pursuit of power is almost always some kind of derangement, no matter how good your intentions. *Blind Giant* is about that derangement and its hallmarks: misogyny, guilt, aggression, egomania, sexual conquest, self-pity, paranoia, anger, righteousness, a singular and unbending point of view… I could give present examples of all this but it would only give more attention to a long list of petty men throwing giant tantrums at public expense who we're all pretty fed up with already.

And besides, *Blind Giant* is really about the antidotes to this derangement: collective undertakings, shared understandings, feminism, critique, outspokenness, moral leadership, compassion, love, variety of life… A more fragile list, but more necessary for it. I'd like to think that if politics tends to favour the deranged list, the arts and Belvoir in particular can favour this one – another reason to begin my tenure with this play.

Paul Keating likes to point out that the proof of the Hawke-Keating reforms is in the pudding – to paraphrase him: *a new compact between labour and capital which produced 25 years of unbroken economic growth, unmatched in the western world*. The argument is so self-saucing that it's hard to imagine that the last thirty years could have turned out any other way. *Blind Giant* is about the moment when it all began, and the corruption that it entailed. I don't just mean literal corruption – though that too, obviously – I mean the corruption of the very idea of society, of a public good or a greater good. The economics might have worked (that's debatable) but the moral landscape of the country definitely changed. We're still trying to make sense of what happened.

This is a play about how we live together. It works by dramatising what happens when we forget how to live together. It tells the story of a man who came to realise throughout the winter of 1983 that the political party he thought best represented his hopes had chosen instead to dash them. In the face of profound uncertainty he chooses to seek his own power. At the same time it tells the story of a woman who refuses to accept that political power is the only way, or even any kind of way, to make sense of disorder – who knows that justice and freedom and choice must be worked out on the ground, every day, at the human scale, in a manner by which their benefits are available not just to the winners, but to everyone…

Eamon Flack

Yael Stone

DAY SYDNEY, NIGHT SYDNEY

Tom Wright

What happens to a city over time? Buildings, streets, harbours, gardens change, if slowly. Fashions mutate. Names change; at *A bourgeois party. A balcony overlooking the Harbour* the wines are called Chablis, Burgundy, Moselle. Everyone smokes. The people sound the same, look almost the same, but inside they are transforming frantically. Technology redefines everything. A Sydney without emails or mobiles feels like an unreliable memory. A Sydney with steel mills? A Sydney actually *making* something, not just shifting notional capital around? *The sound of a telex machine* – what was that?

But cities remember, keep their past inside. Some of it is repressed, some easy to recall.

On one level *The Blind Giant is Dancing* is very much a play of its time, and that gives it so much of its power. As its author remarks in this program, these Sydney men and women are so *alive*. It is the energy of being at the cusp, but also the energy of a people with something at stake. Explicit in the play is the way ideology and resistance can move through generations; the dead, the old, the on-their-way-out are enlisted in the endless fight to hold onto something that's actually ours. The young, the unborn wait in the wings; the costumes will change but the set will be similar. And the city keeps pulsing.

A few years before this play, a woman campaigning against corrupt obliteration of communities disappeared from a Kings Cross cellar. A bomb exploded on George Street outside a multinational hotel. While this play was being written a man went for a meeting with police in Chippendale and ended up shot in a gutter. Shortly after this play's premiere, the city (like the rest of the country) seemed to temporarily lose its marbles over a wealthy Perth shyster winning a yacht race in America. A few years after this, a woman floated in a pond in Centennial Park, having made the fatal mistake of speaking about this city's secrets in the light of day. The steady atomisation of life was happening everywhere, and at the same time nowhere. If a street needed to be saved from venal cleansing, green bans could be applied. But while streets were saved, less tangible things were being wiped out.

A complicated city, emerging from provincial outpost into that horrifying construct: a 'World City', another market hub. We are here now, and we're there too. The southerly buster still blows after the heat. The beer is still cool on the verandah. The currawongs and orb-weavers still lurk in the bushes. But how do we remember who we were? How do we bear witness to the arguments of our parents and draw fresh conclusions? Maybe through great plays of the city, like this one.

Tom Wright is an Artistic Associate at Belvoir.

BIOGRAPHIES

STEPHEN SEWELL Writer

Stephen is one of Australia's most celebrated and experienced writers. He is well known for his film and theatre work, including the AFI Award-winning film script of *The Boys* as well as plays such as *Dreams in an Empty City*, *It Just Stopped*, *Three Furies*, *The Gates of Egypt*, *Hate*, *Sisters*, *Traitors* and *Kandahar Gate*. Stephen's play *Myth, Propaganda and Disaster in Nazi Germany and Contemporary America* won an AWGIE for Best Play, Victorian Premier's Literary Award for Literature, NSW Premier's Literary Award for Literature and the Victorian Green Room Award for Best New Play. Stephen has worked as a playwright, screenwriter, dramaturg and script editor, as well as a theatre and film director. His extensive film career includes work as screenwriter and script editor on some of Australia's most significant films, such as *True Love and Chaos* and *Chopper*. He has recently written and directed his first feature film *Embedded*, starring Laura Gordon and Nick Barkla, to be released in 2016, and is now casting his second feature, *Wolf*. Stephen is Head of Writing for Performance at the National Institute of Dramatic Art.

EAMON FLACK Director

Eamon is Belvoir's Artistic Director. He was born in Singapore and grew up in Singapore, Darwin, Brisbane and Cootamundra. He trained as an actor at WAAPA from 2001 to 2003 and has since worked as a director, actor, writer and dramaturg all over the country, from Milikapiti on the Tiwi Islands to Melbourne and Perth. For Belvoir, Eamon has directed *Ivanov*, *Angels in America Parts One and Two*, *The Glass Menagerie*, *Babyteeth*, *As You Like It*, *Mother Courage and Her Children*, *Once in Royal David's City* and *The End*. He co-adapted Ruby Langford Ginibi's memoir *Don't Take Your Love to Town* with Leah Purcell, and co-devised *Beautiful One Day* with artists from ILBIJERRI, version 1.0 and Palm Island. His dramaturgy credits for Belvoir include *Neighbourhood Watch*, *The Wild Duck*, *Brothers Wreck* and *The Book of Everything*. His adaptations include Chekhov's *Ivanov*, Gorky's *Summerfolk* and Sophocles' *Antigone*. *Ivanov* won four 2015 Sydney Theatre Awards, including Best Mainstage Production and Best Direction. Eamon's productions of *The Glass Menagerie* and *Angels in America* both won Best Play at the Helpmann Awards. Later in 2016 Eamon will be directing *The Great Fire* and *Twelfth Night* at Belvoir.

MICHAEL DENKHA Mr Carew

Michael graduated from the National Institute of Dramatic Art in 1995. He has appeared in *The Gates of Egypt* (Belvoir); *Edmond* (B Sharp); *A Streetcar Named Desire* (Sydney Theatre Company, US tour); *King Lear, Cyrano de Bergerac* (Sydney Theatre Company); *The Pugilist Specialist* (Darlinghurst Theatre Company); *Coriolanus* (Bell Shakespeare); *Road, Three Strikes* (Tamarama Rock Surfers); *Missing the Bus to David Jones* (Performing Lines); *Permission to Spin* (Merrigong Theatre Company); and *The Year of Living Dangerously* (Black Swan State Theatre Company). His feature films include *Down Under, 6 Days, The Combination, The Nothing Men, Mask II, Stealth, Get Rich Quick* and *Risk*. For television Michael has appeared in *Here Come the Habibs!, The Principal, The Code, Catching Milat, Rake, Black Comedy, The Devil's Playground, Wednesday Night Fever, At Home with Julia, All Saints, East West 101, Chandon* and *Home and Away* among others.

IVAN DONATO Ramon Gris

Ivan is a National Institute of Dramatic Art graduate. His stage credits include *A Christmas Carol* (Belvoir); *Hamlet* (Bell Shakespeare); *Macbeth, Machinal* (Sydney Theatre Company); *Blood Wedding* (Malthouse Theatre); *Macbeth* (Bell Shakespeare); *Strange Attractor* (Griffin Theatre Company); *Othello* (Sport for Jove); *Belongings, Bang* (White Box); *Cherry Smoke* (Old Fitz); *The Jungle* (Darlinghurst Theatre); *The Berryman* (HotHouse Theatre); and *Orestes 2.0* (Cry Havoc). Ivan was also part of Bell Shakespeare's 2011 Learning Ensemble.

DALE FERGUSON Set & Costume Designer

Dale has designed many Belvoir productions including *Radiance, Brothers Wreck, Summer of the Seventeenth Doll, Neighbourhood Watch, The Seagull, Measure for Measure, The Power of Yes, Antigone, Exit the King, Peribanez, The Sapphires, The Chairs, The Dreamers, The Marriage of Figaro, The Judas Kiss* and *A Cheery Soul*. *The Judas Kiss* was remounted in the West End in 2013 following a regional tour in the UK. Dale's other credits for theatre include *Menagerie* (Daniel Schlusser Ensemble); *Les Liaisons Dangereuses, The Convict's Opera, The 25th Annual Putnam County Spelling Bee, Summer Rain* (Sydney Theatre Company); *The Weir, The Speechmaker, The Crucible, Top Girls, Life Without Me, The Drowsy Chaperone, God of Carnage, August: Osage County, The History Boys, Don's Party, The Female of the Species* (Melbourne Theatre Company); *The Riders* (Opera Victoria); *Timeshare, Dance of Death, Night on Bald Mountain, Woman-Bomb* (Malthouse Theatre); *Rapture, Nightfall* (Playbox Theatre Company); and the Sydney productions of *Anything Goes, An Officer and a Gentleman* (GFO); *Titanic the Musical* (Seabiscuit Productions); and *The Rocky Horror Picture Show* (New Theatricals). For opera, Dale has designed *Otello* (Cape Town Opera/Opera Queensland/Western Australian Opera); *A Midsummer Night's Dream* (Houston Grand Opera/Lyric Opera of Chicago/Canadian Opera Company); *Ariadne auf Naxos, The Marriage of Figaro* (Welsh National Opera); *The Marriage of Figaro* and *Eugene Onegin* (Opera Australia). Dale received a Helpmann Award for *August: Osage County*, and Tony and Drama Desk nominations for the Broadway season of Belvoir's *Exit the King*.

Yael Stone

Dan Spielman
Ben Wood

Michael Denkha
Genevieve Lemon

VERITY HAMPSON Lighting Designer

Verity is a National Institute of Dramatic Art graduate with over 10 years' experience as a lighting and projection designer. For Belvoir Verity's designs include *Ivanov, Is This Thing On?, Small and Tired, The Business, That Face* and *The Gates of Egypt*. She has designed over 70 theatre productions, working with some of Australia's most talented directors and choreographers. For television Verity has been a lighting director for the ABC's *Live at the Basement* and *The Roast*. She was awarded the Mike Walsh Fellowship in 2012 which took her to Broadway to work with projection designers 59 Productions. Verity was the winner of the 2013 Sydney Theatre Award for Best Mainstage Lighting Design for her work on *Machinal* at Sydney Theatre Company.

ANDREW HENRY Bruce Fitzgerald

Andrew is an alumnus from the School at Steppenwolf and a founding member and the Artistic Director of Red Line Productions. His theatre credits include *Of Mice and Men* (Sport for Jove); *Orphans, Howie The Rookie* (Red Line Productions); *Freud's Last Session* (QPAC); *Europe* (Seymour Centre); *All My Sons* (Eternity Playhouse); *Frankenstein* (Ensemble Theatre); *Reasons To Be Pretty* (Darlinghurst Theatre Company); *The Schelling Point* (Tamarama Rock Surfers); and *The Chronic-ills of Robert Zimmerman aka Bob Dylan* (Tamarama Rock Surfers). Andrew's television credits include *Janet King, Secret City, The Code, The Cut* and *Love Child*. Andrew won a 2014 Sydney Theatre Award for the Best Actor in a Leading Role in an Independent Production for *Howie the Rookie*.

EMMA JACKSON Janice / Jane / Robin

Emma's career has spanned theatre, film and TV since her graduation from the National Institute of Dramatic Art. For Belvoir she has appeared in three seasons of *Food*, including an extensive national tour. Her other credits include *Fool for Love* (B Sharp/Savage Productions); *The Long Way Home* (Sydney Theatre Company), *Nothing Personal, Let the Sunshine* (Ensemble Theatre); *Dead Man's Cellphone* (Melbourne Theatre Company); and *Stoning Mary* (Griffin Theatre Company). Emma won the Marten Bequest Travelling Scholarship in 2006 and relocated to New York to train with the SITI Co and intern with The Wooster Group. In the US Emma appeared in *The Bird, Reader, Windows* and *Bed* (One Year Lease Theatre Company, New York); and *C4 The Chekhov Project* (Prospect Theatre, New York). She also performed in *Reasonable Doubt* (Theatre Tours International) in London and at the Edinburgh Festival. Emma's screen credits include *The Killing Field, Crownies, Killing Time, The Alice* and *Rescue*.

RUSSELL KIEFEL Doug Fitzgerald / Sir Leslie Harris

Russell has previously performed for Belvoir in *Buried City*, *The Business*, *The Power of Yes*, *The Gates of Egypt*, *Ray's Tempest*, *Stuff Happens*, *Our Lady of Sligo*, *The Spook*, *Run Rabbit Run*, *The Alchemist*, *The Tempest*, *The Blind Giant is Dancing* (1995 production) and *Hamlet*. His other theatre credits include *Travelling North*, *Our Town*, *A Streetcar Named Desire*, *Self Esteem*, *Racing Demon*, *St Joan*, *Macbeth*, *Sydney Stories* (Sydney Theatre Company); *The Alchemist*, *Hamlet*, *King Lear* (Bell Shakespeare); *And No More Shall We Part*, *King Tide*, *Rabbit* (Griffin Theatre Company); *American Buffalo*, *Simpatico*, *Twelfth Night*, *Hotel Sorrento* (Queensland Theatre Company); *A Winter's Tale*, *Twelfth Night*, *The Blind Giant is Dancing*, *Mother Courage* (State Theatre Company of South Australia); *Nowhere* and *Insouciance* (Playbox). After graduating from NIDA in 1974, Russell made his film debut in an early Gillian Armstrong film, *The Singer and the Dancer*, and has since appeared in Australian classics such as *Breaker Morant*, *Children of the Revolution*, *Radiance*, *Dogwatch* and *Fresh Air*. His most recent film role was in *Son of a Gun*. Russell's television credits include *Secret City*, *Neighbours*, *Childhood's End*, *Schapelle*, *Tricky Business*, *Spirited*, *Rake*, *Underbelly: The Golden Mile*, *A Model Daughter: the Killing of Caroline Byrne*, *Chandon Pictures*, *Chifley's Fifty Days*, *To Catch a Killer*, *McLeod's Daughters*, *All Saints* and *Fireflies*.

GENEVIEVE LEMON Eileen Fitzgerald

Previously for Belvoir **Genevieve** has appeared in *Seventeen*, *Death of a Salesman* and *The Cosmonaut's Last Message*. Her other theatre credits include *Billy Elliot* (Working Title, London & Sydney seasons); *Priscilla Queen of the Desert* (Priscilla on Stage); *Noises Off*, *Summer Rain*, *Victory*, *The Republic of Myopia*, *Harbour*, *Hanging Man*, *Morning Sacrifice* (Sydney Theatre Company); *Broken Glass* (Ensemble Theatre); and *Piaf* (Melbourne Theatre Company.) She also appeared in the Australian premieres of *Steaming*, *Steel Magnolias* and *My Brilliant Divorce*. Genevieve's television credits include *Redfern Now*, *The Secret River*, *Rake*, *Top of the Lake*, *After the Beep*, *Three Men and a Baby Grand*, *Heartland*, *Neighbours* and *Prisoner*. Her film credits include *The Dressmaker*, *The Water Diary*, *Suburban Mayhem*, *Soft Fruit*, *Billy's Holiday*, *The Piano* and *Sweetie*. Genevieve has performed in the Wharf Revue and many other cabarets in Australia and London, and has produced an album of her Sydney Opera House concert, *Angels in the City*. Genevieve received Helpmann, Sydney Theatre Critics Circle and Green Room awards for her role in *Billy Elliot*, and received AFI nominations for her roles in *Suburban Mayhem* and *Sweetie*. For her role in *Seventeen*, Genevieve was nominated for a 2015 Sydney Theatre Award in the Best Ensemble category.

GEOFF MORRELL Michael Wells

Geoff is one of Australia's most prolific stage and screen actors. His stage credits include *Ruben Guthrie*, *The Tempest* (Belvoir); *Australia Day*, *Rabbit*, *Away*, *Oleanna*, *Tom and Viv*, *The Seagull* (Sydney Theatre Company); *Vere* (Sydney Theatre Company/State Theatre Company of South Australia); *King Lear* (State Theatre Company of South Australia); *Macbeth* (Classical Theatre Co); *Man of La Mancha* (Gordon Frost Organisation); *Speaking in Tongues* (Griffin Theatre Company); *Blithe Spirit* (Melbourne Theatre Company); and *Things We Do for Love* (Marian Street Theatre). Geoff's notable roles in film include *Ten Empty*, *Ned Kelly*, *Lucky Miles*, *The View from Greenhaven Drive*, *Coffin Rock*, *Gimme Shelter* and *The Mule*. His lead television roles include *Cloudstreet*, *Grass Roots*, *Small Time Gangster* and *Blue Heelers*; and guest roles in the series *Miss Fisher's Murder Mysteries*, *Rake*, *Winners and Losers*, *The Secret Life of Us*, *Stingers*, *Home and Away*, *Farscape*, *Curtin*, *Please Like Me* and *Serangoon Road*. Most recently Geoff has appeared in *Catching Milat*, *8MMM*, *The Code* and the film *Red Christmas*. Geoff will also be appearing in *The Great Fire*, next in the Upstairs Theatre at Belvoir.

ZAHRA NEWMAN Rose Draper

A 2008 graduate of the Victorian College of the Arts, **Zahra**'s theatre credits include *Ivanov*, *Private Lives* (Belvoir); *The Government Inspector* (Belvoir/Malthouse Theatre); *Love and Information* (Malthouse Theatre/Sydney Theatre Company); *As You Like It* (Bell Shakespeare); *The Effect*, *The Mountaintop*, *The Cherry Orchard*, *Clybourne Park*, *Richard III*, *The Drowsy Chaperone*, *Rockabye* (Melbourne Theatre Company); *An Officer and A Gentleman – The Musical* (GFO); *Menagerie* (Daniel Schlusser Ensemble/NEON Festival); and *Elektra* (Fraught Outfit). Zahra was awarded the Green Room Award for Best Actress for her critically acclaimed national tour of *Random* (Melbourne Theatre Company/Sydney Opera House/Brisbane Powerhouse) and has been nominated for Helpmann Awards for Best Actress for *The Mountaintop* and Best Supporting Actress for *The Government Inspector*. Her film and TV credits include *Rush*, the feature film *Truth*, the miniseries *Childhood's End* and the TV pilot *Bleak*. Zahra is a proud member of MEAA.

GRACE NYE-BUTLER Assistant Stage Manager

Grace graduated from the Western Australian Academy of Performing Arts (WAAPA) with an Advanced Diploma of Stage Management. For Belvoir Grace has stage managed *The Wizard of Oz*, *Stories I Want to Tell You in Person*, was assistant stage manager on *Coranderrk* and *Medea* and for the early rehearsals of *Elektra / Orestes*, and was seconded to *Death of a Salesman*. Grace's other assistant stage manager credits include the national tours of *Hamlet* and *Henry V* (Bell Shakespeare); and *Boundary Street* at the Brisbane Festival (Black Swan State Theatre Company). At WAAPA Grace was selected to manage the LINK Dance Company's international tour to France and The Netherlands in 2011. Grace has been involved with Sydney Festival, Optus RockCorps, and Pacific Opera's *Cloudstreet*.

Zahra Newman

Andrew Henry

DAN SPIELMAN Allen Fitzgerald

Dan's stage performances include *A Golem Story, Knives in Hens, The Ham Funeral, The Journal of The Plague Year* (Malthouse Theatre); *The Seagull* (Melbourne Theatre Company); *The Cherry Orchard, The Cripple of Inishmaan* (Sydney Theatre Company); *A Midsummer Night's Dream, Art of War, The Season at Sarsaparilla, The Bourgeois Gentleman, The Lost Echo* and *Mother Courage and Her Children* as a founding member of Sydney Theatre Company's Actors Company; and more than a dozen productions for the Keene/Taylor Theatre from 1998 to 2002. Most recently he starred in *Macbeth* for Bell Shakespeare. Dan has appeared in some of Australia's leading television shows including *The Code, Miss Fisher's Murder Mysteries, Offspring, Raw FM, Blue Heelers, Wildside, Stingers, Farscape, The Secret Life of Us, Satisfaction, Mary Bryant, My Place* and *Darwin's Brave New World*, as well as the ABC telemovie *An Accidental Soldier*. Dan made his feature film debut in *One Perfect Day*, for which he was nominated for an AFI Award for Best Actor and an IF Award for Best Actor. His follow-up performance in *Tom White* earned him a Film Critics Circle Award for Best Supporting Actor and an AFI Award nomination for Best Supporting Actor. In 2011 Dan was seen in *The Hunter*, alongside Willem Dafoe and Sam Neill. He has also featured in a number of short films including *The Lighter, The Director, The Pitch* and *The Date*, which earned him a Tropfest Best Actor Award. Dan received an AACTA Award nomination for Best Lead Actor in a Television Drama for *The Code* and recently wrapped on the second series.

MELANIE STANTON Stage Manager

Melanie completed a Bachelor of Fine Arts in Technical Production (Theatre) at Queensland University of Technology in 2003. She returns to Belvoir after stage managing *Conversation Piece* (Belvoir/Lucy Guerin Inc) both in Australia and the European tour. She also stage managed a national tour of *Food* (Belvoir/Force Majeure) in 2013. Melanie has worked for Queensland Music Festival, Brisbane Festival, St Kilda Festival, Melbourne Festival, Melbourne Commonwealth Games Opening and Closing Ceremonies, the Doha Asian Games Opening and Closing Ceremonies, as well as local and touring stage management roles for Malthouse Theatre, Victorian Opera and Chunky Move. While based in the UK throughout 2013-2014, Melanie worked for Assembly Festival (Edinburgh Festival Fringe) and on a UK tour of *Kindertransport* (Hall & Childs). Last year Melanie had roles with the Opening and Closing Ceremonies of the Baku 2015 European Games, and the 44th UAE National Day event in Abu Dhabi.

Russell Kiefel

Dan Spielman
Emma Jackson

Ivan Donato

YAEL STONE Louise Kraus

Yael graduated from the National Institute of Dramatic Art in 2006. For Belvoir she has appeared in *As You Like It, Summer of the Seventeenth Doll, The Diary of a Madman* (Sydney & New York tour), *The Book of Everything* (Sydney & New York tour) and *Scorched*. Her other theatre credits include *Tommy* (Hal Willner productions/ Adelaide Festival); *A Golem Story* (Malthouse Theatre); *Honour, Elling, Frankenstein* (Sydney Theatre Company); *Harbinger* (Brink Productions); Ladybird (B Sharp/Small Things Productions); *Stoning Mary* (Griffin Stablemates /Frogbattleship); and *The Kid* (Griffin Theatre Company). Yael's television credits include Netflix's multi award-winning and internationally acclaimed *Orange Is the New Black* (seasons 1–4), *High Maintenance, Childhood's End, Spirited* (seasons 1 & 2), *All Saints* and *The Farm*. Her film credits include *Wilde Wedding, Falling, West* and *Me, Myself, I*. In 2015 Yael won a Screen Actors Guild Award as part of the *Orange Is the New Black* ensemble, and is nominated in the same category in 2016. She won the 2009 Sydney Theatre Award for Best Actress in a Supporting Role for *The Kid* and Best Newcomer for her roles in both *The Kid* and *Frankenstein*. Yael received Helpmann Award nominations for her roles in *Scorched, The Book of Everything* and *The Diary of a Madman*. Yael has been a proud member of Equity since 1998.

STEVE TOULMIN Composer & Sound Designer

Steve's composition and/or design credits include *Jasper Jones, Ivanov, La Traviata, Blue Wizard, Radiance, Is This Thing On?, 20 Questions, The Baulkham Hills African Ladies Troupe, The Seed, Scorched* (Belvoir); *All The Sex I've Ever Had* (Sydney Festival); *Little Mercy, Edward Gant's Amazing Feats of Loneliness* (Sydney Theatre Company); *The Bleeding Tree, Beached, A Hoax* (Griffin Theatre Company); *Great Falls, Liberty Equality Fraternity, Circle Mirror Transformation* (Ensemble); *That Face* (Queensland Theatre Company); *Tender Napalm, Julius Caesar* and *Hamlet* (La Boite Theatre Company). As a songwriter and music producer Steve has worked with artists including Megan Washington, Ricki-Lee Coulter and Samantha Jade.

BEN WOOD Bob Lang

Ben studied at the Australian Theatre for Young People (ATYP). His theatre credits include *Rupert* (Daniel Sparrow Productions); *Henry 4, Twelfth Night, The Duchess of Malfi* (Bell Shakespeare); *The Aliens* (Redline Productions); *Ghost Stories* (Sydney Opera House); *A Midsummer Night's Dream, As You Like It* (Sport for Jove); *What the Umbrella Did Next, 17, 3 Little Fears, Skate* (ATYP); *La Dispute, The Europeans, Bad Jazz* (Darlinghurst Theatre Company); *The Removalists, Empire: Terror on the High Seas, Soldier/Thief* (Tamarama Rock Surfers); *Hamlet* (Harlos Productions); *Macbeth* (Wildfire Theatre Company); *Her Holiness, Love Field* and *The Crucible* (Bakehouse Theatre Company). Ben's film credits include *Hitchhiker, The Kangaroo Guy, The Trophy Thief, Father's Day, My Mind's Own Melody, Footy Legends, Wall Boy, Dream the Life* and *Strangerland*. His television credits include *All Saints, Underbelly 3: The Golden Mile, Packed to the Rafters, Rescue: Special Ops, A Model Daughter, My Place, Redfern Now* and *Janet King*, among others. Ben is a proud member of Equity.

BELVOIR STAFF

18 Belvoir Street, Surry Hills NSW 2010
Email mail@belvoir.com.au Web belvoir.com.au
Administration (02) 9698 3344 Facsimile (02) 9319 3165 Box Office (02) 9699 3444

Artistic Director
Eamon Flack
Executive Director
Brenna Hobson
Deputy Executive Director & Head of Development
Nathan Bennett

BELVOIR BOARD
Anne Britton
Mitchell Butel
Andrew Cameron (Chair)
Luke Carroll
Tracey Driver
Eamon Flack
Brenna Hobson
Ian Learmonth
Olivia Pascoe
Peter Wilson

BELVOIR ST THEATRE BOARD
Trefor Clayton (Chair)
Stuart McCreery
Angela Pearman
Sue Rosen
Nick Schlieper
Mark Seymour
Kingsley Slipper
Susan Teasey

ARTISTIC & PROGRAMMING
Associate Producer
Luke Cowling
Associate Director – Literary
Anthea Williams
Artistic Associate
Tom Wright

EDUCATION
Education Manager
Jane May
Acting Education Coordinator
Hannah McBride

ADMINISTRATION
Artistic Administrator
John Woodland
Trainee Administration Coordinator
Anthony Blanch

FINANCE & OPERATIONS
Head of Finance & Operations
Kate Chalker
Company Accountant
Komal Rabadiya
Accounts Administrator
Susan Jack
IT & Operations Manager
Jan S. Goldfeder

BOX OFFICE
Box Office Manager
Tanya Ginori-Cairns
Assistant Box Office Manager
Andrew Dillon
Subscriptions Manager
Jason Lee

FRONT OF HOUSE
Front of House Manager
Ohmeed Ahi
Assistant Front of House Manager
Scott Pirlo

DEVELOPMENT
Acting Philanthropy Manager
Charlotte Bradley
Development Coordinator
Aimee Timmins

MARKETING
Marketing Manager
Amy Goodhew
Marketing & Digital Content Coordinator
Jacqueline Mcleish
Publications Manager
Gabrielle Bonney
Publicity & Public Affairs Manager
Elly Baxter

PRODUCTION
Head of Production
Warren Sutton
Production Coordinator
Eliza Maunsell
Technical Manager
Will Jacobs
Resident Stage Manager
Luke McGettigan
Staging & Construction Manager
Penny Angrick
Staging & Construction Assistant
TBA
Costume Coordinator
Judy Tanner
Senior Technician
Caitlin Porter

SUNDAY FORUM

It's not just about seeing the shows – there's a conversation to be had as well.

Sometimes the most fascinating part of a theatre-going experience is delving into not just *what* it's about, but *how* it's being done. At Belvoir's Sunday Forums we bring artists and audiences together to peel back the surface and see what's really going on in our plays. We'll chew over the social, the political and the familial. We'll discuss the play, the production – and the glorious space between the two. Serious one month, feisty the next – but always intriguing and you're *always* invited.

We hold a Forum for each of our Upstairs productions. The panellists are made up of both theatre artists and invited guests; you can check our website in advance for a run-down of who will be on and the topic of conversation. You'll have the chance to ask questions, meet your fellow audience members and continue the discussion informally with us in the bar afterwards.

Sunday Forums are **FREE** but we'd like you to book so we can save you a spot. Book online at **belvoir.com.au/sundayforum** or call Box Office. Tweet while you listen using #sundayforum

The Blind Giant is Dancing
3pm, 20 March

The Great Fire
3pm, 8 May

The Events
3pm, 12 June

Back at the Dojo
3pm, 17 July

Twelfth Night
3pm, 4 September

The Drover's Wife
3pm, 16 October

Faith Healer
3pm, 27 November

Girl Asleep
3pm, 18 December

Dan Spielman

Theatricality. Variety of life. Faith in humanity.

Belvoir is a theatre company on a side street in Surry Hills, Sydney. We share our street with a park and a public housing estate, and our theatre is in an old industrial building. It has been, at various times, a garage, a sauce factory, and the Nimrod Theatre. When the theatre was threatened with redevelopment in 1984, more than 600 people formed a syndicate to buy the building and save the theatre. Thirty years later, Belvoir St Theatre continues to be home to one of Australia's most celebrated theatre companies.

In its early years Belvoir was run cooperatively. It later rose to international prominence under first and longest-serving Artistic Director Neil Armfield and continued to be both wildly successful and controversial under Ralph Myers. Belvoir is a traditional home for the great old crafts of acting and story in Australian theatre. It is a platform for voices that won't otherwise be heard. And it is a gathering of outspoken ideals. In short: theatricality, variety of life, and faith in humanity.

At Belvoir we gather the best theatre artists we can find, emerging and established, to realise an annual season of works – new Australian plays, Indigenous works, re-imagined classics and new international writing. Our work travels the country and we regularly take our productions overseas. Audiences remember many landmark productions including *Angels in America*, *Brothers Wreck*, *The Glass Menagerie*, *Neighbourhood Watch*, *The Wild Duck*, *Medea*, *The Diary of a Madman*, *Death of a Salesman*, *The Blind Giant is Dancing*, *Hamlet*, *Cloudstreet*, *Aliwa*, *The Book of Everything*, *Keating!*, *The Exile Trilogy*, *Exit the King*, *The Sapphires* and *Who's Afraid of Virginia Woolf?*

Belvoir receives government support for its activities from the federal government through the Major Performing Arts Panel of the Australia Council and the state government through Arts NSW. We also welcome and warmly appreciate all philanthropic support.

belvoir.com.au
Artistic Director **Eamon Flack**
Executive Director **Brenna Hobson**

BELVOIR

JASPER JONES
2 JAN – 7 FEB

THE BLIND GIANT IS DANCING
13 FEB – 20 MAR

THE GREAT FIRE
2 APR – 8 MAY

THE EVENTS
12 MAY – 12 JUN

BACK AT THE DOJO
18 JUN – 17 JUL

TWELFTH NIGHT
23 JUL – 4 SEP

THE DROVER'S WIFE
17 SEP – 16 OCT

FAITH HEALER
22 OCT – 27 NOV

GIRL ASLEEP
2 – 24 DEC

THE TRIBE
19 JAN – 7 FEB

HANNAH GADSBY – DOGMATIC
20 – 22 MAY

RUBY'S WISH
21 SEP – 9 OCT

TITLE AND DEED
13 OCT – 6 NOV

2016 SEASON

COME AND SEE SUBSCRIBE NOW
BELVOIR.COM.AU

BELVOIR DONORS

We give our heartfelt thanks to all our donors for their loyal and generous support.

CREATIVE DEVELOPMENT FUND

$10,000+
Andrew Cameron AM & Cathy Cameron **
Sherry-Hogan Foundation*
Kim Williams AM & Catherine Dovey

$5,000 – $9,999
Anonymous (1)
Stephen Allen
Anne Britton**
Hartley Cook*
Louise Herron & Clark Butler**
Peter & Rosemary Ingle*
Helen Lynch AM & Helen Bauer**
Frank Macindoe *
Doc Ross Family Foundation
Victoria Taylor**

$2,000 – $4,999
Neil Armfield AO**
Jill & Richard Berry
Justin Butterworth & Stephen Asher
John Cary
Janet & Trefor Clayton*
Michael Coleman*
Bob & Chris Ernst
Richard Evans
Lisa Hamilton & Rob White
Victoria Holthouse*
David Marr**
David Robb

$500 – $1,999
Helen Argiris
Richard Banks
Chris Collett
Joanna Collins
Linda English
Timothy Hale
Roey Higgs
Michael Hobbs
Stephanie Hutchinson
Angus Hutchinson
Alec Leopold
Janine Perrett*
Steve Rankine
Penelope Seidler
Alenka Tindale
Sheryl Weil

CO-CONSPIRATORS

$10,000+
Gail Hambly**
Anita Jacoby*
David & Jill Pumphrey
Mark Warburton
Peter Wilson
Cathy Yuncken

THE CHAIR'S GROUP

$3,000+
Judge Joe Harman
Marion Heathcote & Brian Burfitt**
Penny Ward*
David & Jennifer Watson**

$1,000 – $2,999
Antoinette Albert**
Jill & Richard Berry
Jillian Broadbent AO**
Chris Brown
Jan Chapman AO & Stephen O'Rourke**
Louise Christie**
Wesley Enoch
Kathleen & Danny Gilbert**
Sophie Guest*
Michael Hobbs*
Hilary Linstead**
Ross McLean & Fiona Beith*
Cajetan Mula (Honorary Member)
Steve & Belinda Rankine
Alex Oonagh Redmond**
Michael Rose & Jo D'Antonio*
Ann Sherry AO*
Kim Williams AM**

2015 B KEEPERS

$5,000+
Robert & Libby Albert**
Ellen Borda*
Constructability Recruitment
Marion Heathcote & Brian Burfitt**
Don & Leslie Parsonage*

$3,000 – $4,999
Anonymous (1)
Bev & Phil Birnbaum**
Anne Britton**
Louise Christie**
Suzanne & Michael Daniel**
Robyn Godlee & Tony Maxwell
Colleen Kane**
S Khouri & D Cross
Chantal & Greg Roger **
Peter & Jan Shuttleworth*

$2,000 – $2,999
Claire Armstrong & John Sharpe**
Dr Brian T. Carey*
Bob & Chris Ernst**
Cary & Rob Gillespie
Peter Graves**
David & Kathryn Groves*
David Haertsch**
John Head**
Jennifer Ledgar & Bob Lim*
Louise Mitchell & Peter Pether
Dr David Nguyen**
Timothy & Eva Pascoe**
Merilyn Sleigh & Raoul de Ferranti

Judy Thomson*
Lynne Watkins & Nicholas Harding*

$1,000 – $1,999
Anonymous (3)
Berg Family Foundation**
Max Bonnell**
Dr Catherine Brown-Watt
Jan Burnswoods*
Mary Jo & Lloyd Capps**
Elaine Chia
Jane Christensen*
Tracey Driver
Jeanne Eve*
Wendy & Andrew Hamlin**
Libby Higgin*
Michael Hobbs*
Avril Jeans**
Kevin & Rosemarie Jeffers-Palmer **
Corinne & Rob Johnston*
Margaret Johnston
A. le Marchant*
Stephanie Lee*
Atul Lele*
Professor Elizabeth More AM**
Jane Munro
K Nomchong SC
Jacqueline & Michael Palmer
Dr Natalie Pelham*
Greeba Pritchard*
David & Jill Pumphrey
Richard & Heather Rasker*
Colleen Roche
Lesley & Andrew Rosenberg*
David Round
Andrew & Louise Sharpe*
Vivienne Sharpe*
Jennifer Smith
Chris & Bea Sochan*
Jeremy Storer & Annabel Crabb
Sue Thomson*
Lisa Hamilton & Rob White
Paul & Jennifer Winch

THE HIVE

$2,500
Anthony & Elly Baxter
Nathan & Yael Bennett
Justin Butterworth & Stephen Asher
Dan & Emma Chesterman
Este Darin-Cooper & Chris Burgess
Joanna Davidson & Julian Leeser
Tracey Driver
Jeremy Goff & Amelia Morgan-Hunn
Piers Grove
Ruth Higgins
Emma Hogan & Kim Hogan
Nicola Marcus & Jeremy Goldschmidt
Bruce Meagher & Greg Waters
G W Outram & F E Holyoake
Olivia Pascoe
Andrew & Louise Sharpe*
Simpsons Solicitors

Michael Sirmai
The Sky Foundation
Peter Wilson & James Emmett

EDUCATION DONORS

$10,000+
Doc Ross Family Foundation
Susie & Nick Kelly
Ian Learmonth & Julia Pincus

$2,000 - $4,999
Anonymous (1)
Andrew Cameron AM & Cathy Cameron**
Estate of the late Angelo Comino
Ari Droga
Matthew Hall
Julie Hannaford*
Judge Joe Harman
Matthew Kidman
Olivia Pascoe**

$500 - $1,999
32 Edward St
Anonymous (8)
Len & Nita Armfield
Art House Gallery
Ian Barnett*
Victor Baskir
David Bennett AO & Anne Bennett
Paul Bide
AB*
Michael & Colleen Chesterman*
Tracey Clancy
Karen Cooper & Simon Tuxen
Tim & Bryony Cox*
Erin Devery
Veronica Espaliat & Ross Youngman
John B Fairfax AO & Libby Fairfax
JoAnna Fisher
Geoffrey & Patricia Gemmell*
Dorothy Hoddinott AO**

Sue Hyde*
Peter & Rosemary Ingle*
Stewart & Jillian Kellie*
Veronica & Matthew Latham
Ruth Layton
Jennifer Ledgar & Bob Lim*
David Marr & Sebastian Tesoriero
Mary Miltenyi
Polese Family
Ateka & Ted Ringrose
Peter & Janet Shuttleworth*
Chris & Bea Sochan*
Jeremy Storer & Annabel Crabb
Kerry Stubbs
Drew Tait
Ingrid Villata
Richard & Sue Walsh
Carolyn Wright
Jason Yetton & Joanne Lam

GENERAL DONORS

$10,000+
Anonymous (1)
Andrew Cameron AM & Cathy Cameron**
Ross Littlewood & Alexandra Curtin*
Helen Lynch Am & Helen Bauer**

$2,000 - $4,999
Anonymous (2)
Baiba Berzins*
Brenna Hobson
Anita Jacoby*
Patricia Novikoff*
Lynne Watkins & Nicolas Harding

$500 - $1,999
Anonymous (5)
Charles & Hannah Alexander
Ian Barnett
Victor Baskir
Christine Bishop
Ian Breden & Josephine Key*

Dr & Mrs Gil Burton
Susan Casali
Michael & Colleen Chesterman*
Lucy Chipkin
Tim & Bryony Cox*
Jane Diamond*
Diane Dunlop*
Elizabeth Fairfax
Jono Gavin
Peter Gray & Helen Thwaites
Priscilla Guest*
Kim Harding & Irene Miller
Harrison & Kate Higgs*
Dorothy Hoddinott AO**
David Jonas & Desmon Du Plessis
Iphygenia Kallinikos
Robert Kidd
Daniel Knight
Wolf Krueger & José Gutierrez*
Frans Lauenstein
Sarah Lawrence*
R S McColl*
Anthony Nugent*
Judy & Geoff Patterson*
Kathirasen Ponnusamy*
Angela Raymond
Leigh Sanderson
Abhijit & Janice Sengupta
Dr Agnes Sinclair
Eileen Slarke & Family*
Andrew Smyth-Kirk
Dr Titia Sprague
Paul Stein
Harvey Stockwoll
Mike Thompson
Suzanne & Ross Tzannes AM*
Jane Uebergang
Chris Vik & Chelsea Albert
Sarah Walters*
Louisa Ward & Tim Coen
Elizabeth Webby AM
Brian & Trish Wright

* 5+ years of giving   ** 10+ years of giving   *** 15+ years of giving

Belvoir is very grateful to accept all donations. Donations over $2 are tax deductible. If you would like to make a donation or would like further information about any of our donor programs please call our Development Team on 02 9698 3344 or email development@belvoir.com.au
List correct at time of printing.

SPECIAL THANKS
We would like to acknowledge Cajetan Mula, Len Armfield and Geoffrey Scharer. They will always be remembered for their generosity to Belvoir.

These people and foundations supported the redevelopment of Belvoir Street Theatre and purchase of our warehouse.
Andrew & Cathy Cameron (refurbishment of theatre & warehouse)
Russell Crowe (Downstairs Theatre & purchase of warehouse)
The Gonski Foundation & The Nelson Meers Foundation (Gonski Meers Foyer)
Andrew & Wendy Hamlin (Brenna's office)
Hal Herron (The Hal Bar)
Geoffrey Rush (redevelopment of theatre)
Fred Street AM (Upstairs Dressing Room)

Thursday night food

From 7.30pm

#SBSFood

VINI

PROUD SUPPORTER OF BELVOIR

ITALIAN FOOD & WINE
3/118 DEVONSHIRE ST (ON HOLT)
SURRY HILLS 9698 5131
TUES + WED 6PM - LATE
THUR + FRI NOON - LATE
SAT 5:30PM - LATE
WWW.VINI.COM.AU

Ticket holders receive complimentary crostini of the day.

Be the first to know what's happening. Grab a 5-issue subscription to Time Out for just $19.95 (RRP $24.75) **and have the best of Sydney delivered straight to your door each month.**

That's 5 issues of Time Out Sydney magazine with free delivery. Head to **www.magshop.com.au/time-out-sydney/H1601ST1**

Price and savings based on RRP of 5 issues of Time Out Sydney magazine. Offer is limited.

Time Out Sydney

Hatrick Catering

PROUD SUPPORTER OF BELVOIR

Caterers for every event ...

www.hatrickcatering.com
info@hatrickcatering.com
0400 648 699

... making your entertaining delicious & easy

the devonshire

the devonshire is pleased to offer Belvoir Patrons any two courses from the a la carte menu for just $49 pp.

Tables for pre-theatre dining are available from 6pm, vacating before 8pm.

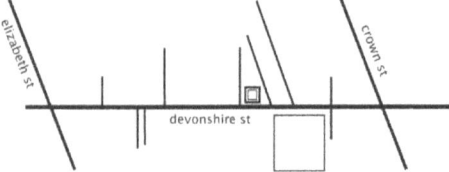

Awarded 1 Chef's hat in the 2014/2015 SMH Good Food Awards

the devonshire, 204 devonshire street, surry hills, 2010

For bookings - 02 9698 9427, devonshiresydney@gmail.com
or www.thedevonshire.com.au

How can our performance help yours?

EY's support of the arts helps institutions to grow, innovate and become more accessible to our local communities.

ey.com/au/arts

The better the question.
The better the answer.
The better the world works.

EY
Building a better
working world

© 2015 Ernst & Young, Australia. All Rights Reserved. Liability limited by a scheme approved under Professional Standards Legislation. S1528806. EDNone. APAC No. A00002474

Baker & McKenzie

Proudly
supporting
Belvoir
since 1994

www.bakermckenzie.com/australia

BELVOIR SPONSORS

MEDIA PARTNERS

MAJOR SPONSORS

IT PARTNER

ASSOCIATE SPONSORS

KEY SUPPORTER

Indigenous theatre at Belvoir supported by The Balnaves Foundation

EVENT SPONSORS

  the devonshire

GOVERNMENT PARTNERS

YOUTH & EDUCATION SUPPORTERS

TRUSTS & FOUNDATIONS

AMP Foundation
Copyright Agency Ltd
Coca-Cola Australia Foundation
Crown Resorts Foundation
Gandevia Foundation
The Greatorex Foundation
Thyne Reid Foundation
Vincent Fairfax Family Foundation

SUPPORTERS

Macquarie Group
Thomas Creative
Time Out Australia

For more information on partnership opportunities please contact our Development team on 02 9698 3344 or email development@belvoir.com.au

Correct at time of printing.

www.ingramcontent.com/pod-product-compliance
Lightning Source LLC
Chambersburg PA
CBHW050016090426
42734CB00021B/3287